MIDGET SUBMARINES 1939–45

CASEMATE | ILLUSTRATED | SPECIAL

CASEMATE | ILLUSTRATED | SPECIAL

MIDGET SUBMARINES 1939–45

INGO BAUERNFEIND

CISS0018

Published in 2025 by
CASEMATE PUBLISHERS
1950 Lawrence Road, Havertown, PA 19083, USA
and
47 Church Street, Barnsley, S70 2AS, UK

Hardback Edition: ISBN 978-1-63624-279-8
Digital Edition: ISBN 978-1-63624-280-4

Design by Battlefield Design
Submarine profiles by Battlefield Design
Printed and bound in the Czech Republic by FINIDR s.r.o.

CASEMATE PUBLISHERS (US)
Telephone (610) 853-9131
Fax (610) 853-9146
Email: casemate@casematepublishers.com
www.casematepublishers.com

CASEMATE PUBLISHERS (UK)
Telephone (0)1226 734350
Email: casemate-uk@casematepublishers.co.uk
www.casematepublishers.co.uk

Title Page: At the end of the war, only 115 Japanese *Type D* boats had been completed, while some 500 more were still incomplete in various shipyards. This type did not see any action. (NHHC)

Contents page: Conning tower of an Italian *Type CB* during World War II with three small windows in its front side. (Former Kriegsmarine)

Contents page background: Salvage of *Ha-18* from Keehi Lagoon east of the entrance to Pearl Harbor in 1960. The fate of the crew is unknown. (NHHC)

Note on the tables: Arrow up (↑) indicates on the surface, and arrow down (↓) indicates submerged.

The Publisher's authorised representative in the EU for product safety is Authorised Rep Compliance Ltd., Ground Floor, 71 Lower Baggot Street, Dublin D02 P593, Ireland.
www.arccompliance.com

Contents

| Introduction

In addition to the large submarines that hunted warships and merchant vessels during World War II, midget submarines and so-called manned (human) torpedoes also saw action. The navies of Germany, Japan, the United Kingdom, and Italy designed and produced these in large numbers. They were used for various purposes, primarily to attack ships in harbors and bays. For example, British midget submarines succeeded in seriously damaging the German battleship *Tirpitz*, moored in a Norwegian fjord. It is also largely unknown that the Japanese attack on Pearl Harbor in 1941 was not only carried out by carrier-based aircraft, but also by five midget submarines. An hour before the air attack, an American destroyer managed to sink one of them in its attempt to enter the harbor. If those responsible in Pearl Harbor had taken the subsequent report seriously, the U.S. Pacific Fleet might have been alarmed, and the attack might have been less devastating.

The *Turtle* was the world's first submersible vessel used in combat. Built in 1775, it was used to attach explosive charges to Royal Navy ships during the American Revolutionary War. However, the attack on the British ship *Eagle* failed. (U.S. Navy)

What Is a Midget Submarine?

Civilian and non-combatant military types are generally called submersibles, which normally operate from surface ships. Today, most early submarines would be considered midget submarines, such as the U.S. Navy's USS *Holland* (SS-1), launched in 1897, and the British Royal Navy's HMS *Holland 1*, launched in 1901. Both were named after the same designer, the Irish engineer John Philip Holland.

There is no firm definition of what constitutes a midget submarine, but typically it is under 150 tons and is operated by a crew of between one and nine. There is almost no onboard accommodation (support and living quarters are provided by a nearby "mother ship"). There is no universal length limit; it all depends on the purpose of the craft. For example, the modern Colombian S.X.506 midget submarine is 75 ft (23 m) long, weighs 70 tons, and has a five-man crew.

The *Alligator* was the first submarine purchased by the U.S. Navy in 1862. It was to attack Confederate warships during the American Civil War but was lost before seeing action. (U.S. Navy)

Ultimately, these weapons were unable to fulfill the expectations placed in them. While the German midget submarines and manned torpedoes were unable to prevent the Allied invasion of Normandy, Japanese units failed in their attempt to halt the American advance in the Pacific. Although Italy and the United Kingdom managed to achieve some respectable successes with their vehicles, it turned out that these weapon systems were unable to have any lasting influence on the course of the conflict. Since the loss rate during various missions, as daring as they were, was often up to 70 or even 100 percent without sinking a single enemy ship, the cost and result were not in any justifiable proportion to each other.

During the war, the United States, France, and the Soviet Union did not develop or extensively use midget submarines, unlike Germany, Japan, Italy, or the United Kingdom. Several key factors influenced this decision, including strategic priorities, operational needs, industrial capacity, and the effectiveness of such vessels in combat.

One of the primary reasons was the strategic focus on larger submarines. The United States in particular prioritized fleet submarines capable of long-range patrols and sustained operations. Therefore, the U.S. Navy relied heavily on its fleet submarines, such as the *Gato*- and *Balao*-classes, which played a critical role in disrupting Japanese shipping in the Pacific. Similarly, the Soviet Union focused on medium and large submarines for operations in the Baltic, Black Sea, and Arctic, rather than smaller, short-range vessels.

The *Hunley* of the Confederate Navy was the world's first submarine that sank an enemy ship, the USS *Housatonic* of the U.S. Navy during the American Civil War, in 1864. (U.S. Navy)

Armament

Additionally, the tactical need for midget submarines was limited. These vessels were primarily used for special operations, harbor raids, and coastal defense missions which were not a priority. The U.S. Navy, being an offensive naval power, did not require small submarines for sabotage missions against enemy harbors, as its primary targets were enemy shipping lanes and naval forces. France, having been occupied by Germany in 1940, had no opportunity to develop or deploy such systems. The Soviet Union, while operating coastal submarines, focused its naval efforts on more conventional engagements, supporting land operations and defending key waterways rather than investing in small-scale sabotage submarines.

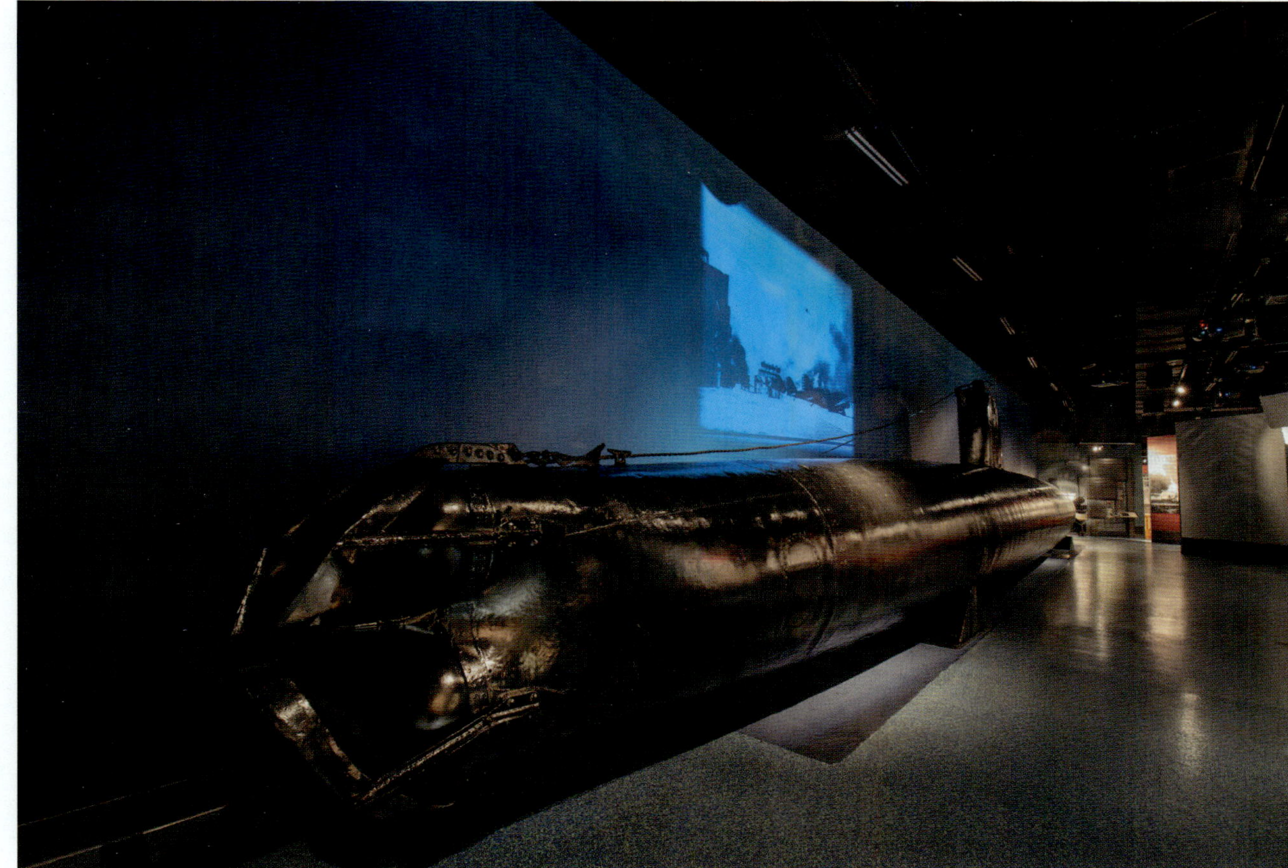

Today, numerous World War II midget submarines are preserved in museums. The boat depicted here is the Japanese *Ha-19* (*Type A*), which took part in the attack on Pearl Harbor in 1941 and is now on display at the National Museum of the Pacific War in Fredericksburg, Texas. (Carol M. Highsmith/U.S. Library of Congress)

Industrial and technological considerations also played a role. The United States had the capacity to build highly capable, large submarines, making midget submarines an unnecessary alternative. The Soviet Union, constrained by wartime production limitations, concentrated its resources on submarines that could make a more significant impact in battle.

Furthermore, lessons from other nations' experiences likely discouraged these powers from investing in midget submarines. The British and Italian navies experimented with them for special operations, such as the British *X-Craft* or the Italian *Maiale* manned torpedoes. Japan and Germany also deployed midget submarines in combat, but with limited success. These vessels suffered high losses and often failed to achieve decisive results in naval battles. The overall lack of effectiveness in such missions may have further reinforced the decision by the U.S., Soviet, and Free French navies to focus on more conventional submarine warfare.

Instead of midget submarines, the United States (and the United Kingdom) developed specialized naval commando units for sabotage and special operations. The United States formed the Office of Strategic Services (OSS) Maritime Unit and the Underwater Demolition Teams, precursors to the Navy SEALs, which became highly effective in covert operations. The Soviet Union also experimented with combat divers for underwater sabotage but did not deploy midget submarines on offensive missions.

Ultimately, the lack of battlefield necessity, combined with the focus on larger submarines and more effective special operations methods, meant that the United States, the Soviet Union (and to a lesser extent the Free French) saw little value in midget submarines during World War II. While they would later explore such technology in the postwar period, these small vessels were not a priority in their wartime naval strategies.

This *Casemate Illustrated Special* features all classes of midget submarines and manned torpedoes built and deployed by Germany, Japan, Italy, and the United Kingdom during World War II, as these nations invested large resources in these weapon systems and expected a great deal from them. This book also features the recovery of various wrecks, including the search for the midget submarines sunk at Pearl Harbor in 1941. The final chapter features the restoration, testing, and successful operation of a German *Biber* midget submarine. The text is accompanied by period photographs as well as exterior and interior images of the various midget submarines and manned torpedoes preserved in museums to this day.

1
Germany

In the years following World War I, and even after the outbreak of the next great conflict in 1939, Germany failed to push ahead with any serious development of small combat equipment in the form of midget submarines, manned torpedoes (human torpedoes), explosive boats, or underwater vehicles for combat divers or swimmers. This was even more surprising as the German Navy, the Reichsmarine (later renamed the Kriegsmarine), had not been allowed to build large surface warships or submarines for a long time due to the Treaty of Versailles, which severely restricted Germany's rearmament after its defeat in 1918. The development of various small combatant vehicles, which the treaty did not mention (and therefore did not prohibit), would therefore have made it possible to build and test a fleet of powerful miniature submarines and other weapon systems as early as the 1920s or 1930s.

Production of *Seehund* midget submarines. Germany only began developing this type of weapon late in the war. (Former Kriegsmarine via Bibliothek für Zeitgeschichte/BfZ)

As the large submarine (fleet submarine) was one of the decisive weapons in the early phase of World War II, its production and deployment were unimpaired by other programs in the navy. The successes of German submarines (known as U-boats derived from the German word *Unterseeboot*—undersea boat) in the Atlantic during the first years of the war also seemed to confirm this theory.

In addition, the use of small and very small submarines with limited seaworthiness and short range on the high seas—e.g., in the Battle of the Atlantic—to attack Allied supply convoys to the United Kingdom and the Soviet Union would only have been possible to a very limited extent.

However, a German study carried out in 1941 concluded that the enemy's ever-improving anti-submarine methods would have to be countered with thousands of small or very small submarines, as only a few hundred large U-boats would be as worthless in the struggle for naval supremacy as a few hundred aircraft in the struggle for air supremacy. Therefore, the diversion of the enemy's defenses, i.e., the deployment of numerous units to split up the enemy's naval forces, was to ensure lasting success. The calculation was that a single German U-boat with a displacement of 2,000 tons would not be as effective in a sea area of operation as, for example, 10 boats of 200 tons each or 20 boats of 100 tons each. The enormous number of boats required was therefore to be made possible by mass production processes such as those used in automobile construction. The boats were then to form large "blocking fields" in the target areas to be blocked and join concentrically around the enemy to attack and then disperse again once the target had been destroyed.

For deployment in remote ocean areas, transportation to the area was to be aboard a U-boat "mother ship" or a surface ship. In addition, the small or very small submarines were to take over the protection of their own coastal waters. However, while the leadership of the Kriegsmarine concentrated on the construction and deployment of the large U-boat *Types VII* and *IX* and even pushed ahead with the development of the new and very advanced *Type XXI*, the navies of Japan, Italy, and the United Kingdom were already successfully deploying various small combatant vehicles.

Although the attack by British manned torpedoes on the German battleship *Tirpitz* in 1942 briefly made the Kriegsmarine take notice, it did not initiate any serious measures to create such a weapon system of its own. Nevertheless, a model for a small submarine (midget submarine) with a length of around 82 ft (25 m), known as the *K-Projekt* was built in the same year. Its design was based on Japanese midget submarine that had been used during the attack on Pearl Harbor on December 7, 1941. The project, which was discontinued after a short time, was the first German attempt to investigate the possibilities of small submarines, at least on models.

> Most German midget submarines were developed late in the war in a desperate attempt to stop the Allied invasion of Europe and used later to disrupt their supply lines off the coast. As a result, the Germans used their boats mostly to engage the enemy in open-water attacks rather than harbor penetration.

From 1943, Germany's military situation deteriorated noticeably. In addition to the growing danger of an Allied invasion in the west, the Kriegsmarine's fighting strength had been greatly reduced due to its high U-boat losses in the Atlantic and its already small surface fleet, which was also losing one ship after another. This new situation called for radical measures. At the end of 1943, a successful British attack finally took place on the battleship *Tirpitz* anchored in a Norwegian fjord. During this operation, two British midget submarines of the *X-Craft* type managed to overcome the net barriers and place two mines under the ship, the detonation of which caused extensive damage to the *Tirpitz*. A short time later, the midget submarines that had been sunk by their crews during this operation were recovered and examined by the Germans. This attack and the destruction of the battleship *Scharnhorst* by superior British naval forces in December 1943, which further weakened the fighting capabilities of the German surface fleet, finally prompted the Kriegsmarine to critically examine the possible uses and chances of success of small combat vehicles at sea.

Midget Submarines

Molch

In the spring of 1944, the first midget submarine named *Molch* (newt) was developed for the Kriegsmarine based on the standard G7 torpedo, which was primarily used to arm the large U-boat *Types VII* and *IX*. As large quantities of G7 components were available, these were also used in the construction of the boat's propulsion system. In addition, the large stock of parts made it possible to build the considerable number of units, 393 in total (or less, depending on the source).

Although most *Molch* midget submarines were scrapped after the war, some have survived in museums. (U.S. Naval History and Heritage Command/NHHC)

Design

The hull had a cylindrical shape that tapered toward the stern. The stern section housed the propulsion system and the position for the operator with the controls for diving. While a wheel was used for lateral control, a stick, like the one in an aircraft, was used for depth control. Propulsion was provided by an electric motor located behind the operator with two speed levels for forward travel (slow speed ahead and full speed ahead), but it had no reverse function. Above the operator's position was a small conning tower with a tiny window on each side and a hinged plexiglass canopy, which was used for access and all-round visibility during operation. The approximately 5 ft (1.5 m) long fixed periscope could be tilted 30° to the right and left.

For diving, the *Molch* had a large water ballast tank in its bow section, which reached almost as far as the operator's position. In between was the space for the eight batteries for the 13 hp electric motor and the compressed air cylinders required for emptying the ballast tanks (cells). There was a smaller ballast tank on each side of the control center. As a counterweight to the heavy stern section, the front ballast tank was constantly filled with water. A separate trim tank was in the lower section of this ballast tank to counterbalance the weight of the operator sitting aft. This tank was also used to compensate for changing water density.

The armament of the one-man vehicle consisted of two G7 torpedoes with a diameter of 21 in (53.3 cm). These were mounted on rails at the bottom of both sides of the hull. The two torpedoes were fired by operating a footrest. Some boats were equipped with a radio, a listening device to detect ships in the vicinity, and an automatic course control system.

The cigar-shaped hull had a small conning tower at its rear with a fixed periscope.
(U.S. Navy)

The *Molch*'s armament consisted of two 21 in (53.3 cm) G7 torpedoes.
(U.S. Navy)

However, test runs revealed a weakness: as the ballast tanks were designed as a combination of diving, control, and trim cells, precise adjustment of the trim and ballast was required before each deployment. If the weight or trim changed during deployment, the operator had to take corrective action by moving the controls or flooding the ballast tanks (cells). This could distract him during a mission and thus make him more vulnerable.

Molch Operations

After the transfer of the K-Flottille 411 (Kleinkampfverband-Flottille 411/small combat unit flotilla 411) to Sanremo in Italy, the first attack by 12 *Molch* midget submarines against the Allied landing forces in southern France took place in September 1944. This operation resulted in the loss of 10 boats without an enemy ship being sunk. The two surviving *Molchs* later fell victim to air raids.

During trials, the *Molch* was able to dive to depths of about 200 ft (60m). The outer hull's thickness was 3 mm. The maximum underwater speed was 5 kn and 4.3 kn (5 mph/9.26 kph and 4.9 mph/8 kph) on the surface. The complicated system of ballast tanks made it difficult to control during combat operations. (U.S. Navy)

Between January and April 1945, the K-Flottille 412 fought a hopeless battle against Allied supply shipping in the North Sea, operating from the Dutch coast with small submarines of the *Molch* and *Biber* types. On 102 missions, most of the flotilla, consisting of some 70 boats, were lost, while only seven small enemy ships were sunk, with two others damaged. The number of losses varies depending on the source. The K-Flottille 413, also intended to be stationed in the Netherlands and the K-Flottille 415 stationed in Norway and Denmark did not see any action until the end of the war. Although the Kriegsmarine recognized that the *Molch* was not suitable for frontline operations, it nevertheless demonstrated its qualities as a training boat for more capable midget submarines then under development.

Year/s of construction	1944
Builder/qty completed	Flender-Werke Lübeck/393
Length	35.43 ft (10.8 m)
Beam	5.91 ft (1.8 m)
Electric motor	13 hp
Propeller	1
Speed ↑	4.3 knots (kn)
Speed ↓	5 kn
Displacement	ca. 11 tons
Range ↑	ca. 50 nm at 4.3 kn
Range ↓	ca. 50 nm at 5 kn
Crew	1
Diving depth	200–230 ft (60–70 m)
Armament	2 torpedoes

Hecht

At the end of 1943, two small British midget submarines of the *X-Craft* type succeeded in placing two mines under the German battleship *Tirpitz* moored in a Norwegian fjord, causing major damage to the ship and disabling it for months. The salvage and investigation of the midget submarines, which had been scuttled by their crews during this attack, led to the demand for a two-man boat that could attach a limpet mine to a ship anchored behind a net barrier. With a displacement of 7 tons and a range of 90 nm (104 mi/167 km), this *Type XXVII*, known as the *Hecht* (northern pike) was also to have a small conning tower, a retractable periscope and a gyrocompass.

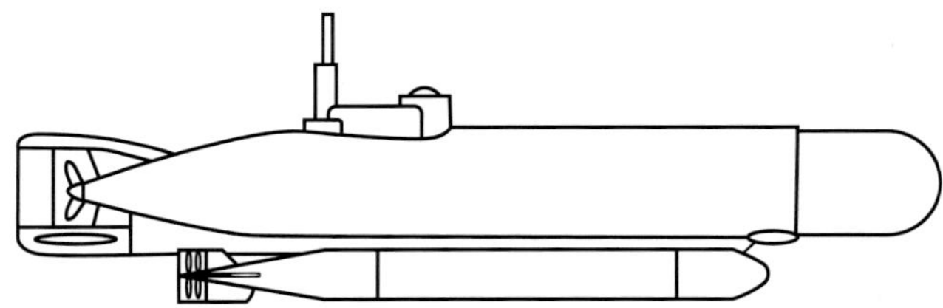

Drawing of the *Hecht*, which only served as a training boat.

Design

However, after the completion of a prototype based on these specifications at the Krupp-Germania Werft (shipyard) in Kiel, the high command of the Kriegsmarine (OKM) changed its requirements: the *Hecht* was now not only to be capable of attacking anchored ships, but also of torpedoing moving targets on the high seas while surfaced. To be suitable for surface operations, it was necessary to modify the hull, which had previously only been designed for underwater use. In addition, a 21 in (53.3 cm) G7 torpedo, which was mounted centrally under the keel of the boat, was to be used as an alternative to the limpet mine. The latter was to be carried in the bow section and could be released from the operator's position. Although there were also trials with other attachments for the transportation of combat divers and their equipment (weapons and inflatable boats), this idea was not implemented. The *Hecht* was no longer to be transported to its operational area by larger ships (as originally planned) but was to operate independently from coasts.

The armament of the *Hecht* consisted of either a 21 in (53.3 cm) G7 torpedo attached under its keel or a magnetic limpet mine in the bow section.

The propulsion consisted of a 12 hp electric motor from AEG for a speed of 6 kn (6.9 mph/11.1 kph) underwater and 5.7 kn (6.6 mph/10.6 kph) on the surface. Depending on the source, some boats are also said to have been powered by 75 hp electric motors, which were originally designed to operate auxiliary bilge pumps in the *Type VII-C* U-boats. During testing, it became apparent that the revised prototype, despite its satisfactory underwater shape, had poor handling characteristics above water, which could not be significantly improved despite modified bow shapes and conning tower cowlings. The officially permitted diving depth of the *Hecht* was approximately 164 ft (50 m), but it could be exceeded by a further 82 ft (25 m).

Although OKM was aware of the *Hecht*'s unsatisfactory sea capabilities, 50 boats were ordered, which were built at Krupp-Germania Werft under the type designation *XXVVII A*. While only the first three boats (*U-2111* to *U-2113*) were fitted with a mine and delivered by June 1944, the other 49 boats completed by August were designed to carry a torpedo. A total of 53 *Hechts*, including the prototype, were completed. However, these were not intended for frontline use from the outset, but purely as training boats for future crews of the more advanced midget submarine *Seehund* (*Type XXVII B*), which was a further development of the *Hecht*. Today, a few *Hecht* boats still exist in museums.

Year/s of construction	1944
Builder/qty completed	Germaniawerft Kiel/53
Length	34.12 ft (10.4 m)
Beam	5.58 ft (1.7 m)
Electric motor	12 hp
Propeller	1
Speed ↑	5.7 kn
Speed ↓	6.0 kn
Displacement	11.8 t
Range ↑	ca. 45 nm at 3 kn
Range ↓	ca. 42 nm at 6 kn (max. 79 nm at 3–4 kn with an additional battery)
Crew	2
Diving depth	160–250 ft (50–75 m)
Armament	1 torpedo or 1 mine

Biber

The design of the *Biber* (beaver) was based to a considerable extent on the British midget submarine *Welman*. One of these boats got caught in a fishing net in November 1943 during its attack on a floating dry dock in the harbor of Bergen in German-occupied Norway. When it was forced to surface, the crew of a German patrol boat was able to capture the *Welman* intact. After its investigation in Germany, some of its design features were incorporated into the concept of the *Biber*.

Artist depiction of a *Biber* operating during World War II. (© Stanislav Hájek/Special Hobby)

A preserved *Biber* in the Technik Museen Speyer, Germany. Several surviving boats are on display in various international museums. (© Technik Museen Sinsheim Speyer)

Preparation of a *Biber* for its mission; it was operated by just one person. (BfZ)

Its prototype, named *Adam*, was built by the Lübeck-based Flenderwerke and underwent its first sea trials in March 1944. During its first dive test, however, the boat sank to the bottom of the Bay of Lübeck. Nevertheless, the pilot was able to save himself. A short time later, *Adam* was raised. After a slight modification of the design, the subsequent diving tests also convinced the commander-in-chief of the Kriegsmarine, Grand Admiral Karl Dönitz, and four further prototypes, 20 training boats, and 300 frontline boats were ordered. They were built at the Flenderwerke and at the Italian Ansaldo shipyard. While the former also fully equipped the boats, the latter only supplied the hulls, which were then fitted out at Klöckner-Humboldt-Deutz in Ulm. To differentiate between them, the boats were given either the company abbreviation LFW or KHD on the inside of their conning towers.

The operational profile of the *Biber* corresponded to that of the *Hecht* in the form of torpedo attacks on anchored and moving ships as well as the placing of mines at various targets. The primary armament of the one-man boat consisted of two G7 torpedoes. These were mounted on rails located in trough-shaped recesses on both sides of the hull. To avoid running aground, which could have damaged the torpedoes or caused a warhead detonation, the boat was equipped with two large skids on the underside of the hull, which protruded slightly lower than the torpedoes. The alternative armament consisted of two mines, which could also be mounted in the trough-shaped recesses.

Series production of the *Biber*. A total of 324 were completed by the end of World War II. (BfZ)

In contrast to the two previous midget submarine types *Molch* and *Hecht*, the *Biber* had a sharp and shark-like bow section to ensure good surface handling. Various model tests and trials with prototypes of the *Molch* and the *Hecht* had shown that their easy-to-build teardrop-shaped hulls with a cylindrical bow had good underwater handling characteristics but suffered from trim problems on the surface.

The pressure hull, made of 3 mm thick sheet steel, consisted (from front to back) of the bow compartment, the forward ballast tank (diving cell), the battery compartment with four batteries, the operator's position (control room) with the steering system, the combustion engine, the electric motor, the stern compartment, and the rear ballast tank (diving cell). A small conning tower with plexiglass windows was located above the control room. It had a hatch through which the pilot could enter or leave the boat. The control room also contained the fixed periscope, a snorkel for the oxygen supply to the combustion engine, the steering system and various operating elements, the four compressed air cylinders for blowing out the tank, an oxygen breathing apparatus, and a bilge pump.

The *Biber*'s armament consisted of two 21 in (53.3 cm) G7 torpedoes. (U.S. Navy)

Due to the lack of available diesel engines, the propulsion for operating on the surface consisted of a 2.5 l Otto engine from the Opel Blitz truck with 32 hp, which gave the *Biber* a speed of 6.5 kn (7.5 mph/12 kph). Due to the dangerous exhaust fumes, the engine was located behind a gas-tight bulkhead directly behind the operator's seat. Behind the combustion engine was a 13 hp GL 231/7.5 SSW electric motor built by the Siemens-Schuckertwerke, enabling the boat to reach 5.3 kn (6.1 mph/9.8 kph) underwater. The range with the combustion engine on the surface was 100 nm (115 mi/185 km) at 6.5 kn (7.5 mph/12 kph) and with the electric motor submerged only 8.5 nm (9.8 mi/15.7 km) at 5.3 kn (6.1 mph/9.8 kph). At a silent running speed (*Schleichfahrt*) of 2.5 kn (2.9 mph/4.6 kph), the *Biber* could cover 8 nm (9.2 mi/14.8 km). The boat had no trim or control cells. While the diving cells (ballast tanks) had to be flooded to descend, they had to be blown out again to ascend. For this reason, controlled travel at periscope depth was practically possible. In addition, torpedoes could only be fired while the *Biber* was on the surface. After completing its mission, it could leave the deployment submerged and evade the enemy in the event of an attack.

Year/s of construction	1944
Builder/qty completed	Flender-Werke Lübeck/324
Length	29.66 ft (9.04 m)
Beam	5.25 ft (1.6 m)
Petrol engine	32 hp
Electric motor	13 hp
Propeller	1
Speed ↑	6.5 kn
Speed ↓	5.3 kn
Displacement	6.3 tons
Range ↑	ca. 100 nm at 6.5 kn
Range ↓	ca. 8.5 nm at 5.3 kn
Crew	1
Diving depth	ca. 100 ft (30 m)
Armament	2 torpedoes

The top edge of the *Biber*'s conning tower was about 20 in (52 cm) above the water. In high waves, it could therefore quickly fill up with water and sink when the conning tower hatch was open. (U.S. Navy)

The conning tower had four plexiglass windows (one on each side) to give the pilot a good all-round view. (U.S. Navy)

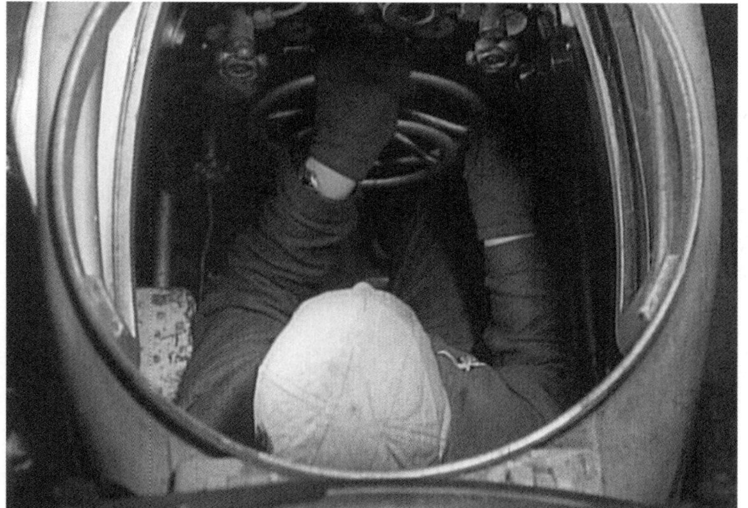

The driver was able to enter the boat through the hatch in the tower. The maximum diving depth was around 100 ft (30 m). (U.S. Navy)

A fake bird's nest attached to the periscope for camouflage purposes. (BfZ)

Closeup view of the conning tower and periscope of the *Biber* preserved at the Technik Museeen Speyer. (© Technik Museeen Sinsheim Speyer)

The 32 hp petrol engine from the Opel *Blitz* truck served as the propulsion while on the surface. (U.S. Navy)

The batteries for the electric motor for submerged operation. (U.S. Navy)

Biber Operations

Although training of the *Biber*'s operators (pilots) was scheduled to last eight weeks, it was carried out in just three to make the boats operational as quickly as possible. Some of the men were given drugs or caffeinated stimulants to keep them awake throughout the one- to two-day voyages. By the end of the war, a total of nine K-flotillas with *Bibers* (Flotillas 261 to 269) had been formed.

The first frontline operation took place on August 30, 1944, from the northern French port of Fécamp to attack Allied ships in the English Channel. Of the 22 boats launched, only 14 were able to leave the harbor. Of these, only two reached their operational area, but were unable to inflict any damage on the enemy.

From December 1944, operations were carried out in the mouth of the Scheldt River, Belgium (access to the North Sea), against Allied shipping en route to Antwerp, to disrupt enemy supplies to the embattled Benelux countries (Belgium, Netherlands, Luxembourg). Of the 18 boats that took part in the first attack on the night of December 22/23, only one returned, while only one Allied cargo ship was sunk. In further operations between December 23 and 25, all 14 boats deployed were lost. The only success was the sinking of the American cargo ship *Alan A. Dale*. On December 27, the accidental launch of a torpedo in Voorneschen in the Netherlands led to the sinking of 11 *Biber* submarines (which were later raised). The bombing by the British Royal Air Force had also damaged the cranes used to lift the boats in and out of the water.

Biber No. 105 held by the Royal Navy Submarine Museum, Gosport, is in working condition and therefore believed to be the only fully operational World War II submarine in existence. It was restored and successfully test-dived in a flooded dry dock in 2003.

Two *Biber* midget submarines mounted on the deck of a German *Type VIIC* U-boat on January 5, 1945, on their way to the Barents Sea to attack an Allied supply convoy or the battleship *Arkhangelsk*. Technical problems thwarted the operation. (BfZ)

In January 1945, the *Type VIIC* U-boats *U-295*, *U-318*, and *U-716* transported several *Biber* midget submarines from Harstad in Norway to the Barents Sea while submerged. From there they were to enter Kola Bay to attack either an Allied supply convoy or the battleship *Arkhangelsk* (originally the British HMS *Royal Sovereign* on loan to the USSR). During the voyage into the Barents Sea, the vibrations of the U-boat power plants led to leaks in the stuffing boxes (seals) of the *Bibers'* drive shafts, causing water to leak into their engine compartments. This incident led to the mission being aborted. It later turned out that neither the battleship nor a convoy had been in port at the time of the planned attack.

Another failed operation took place at the beginning of 1945 from Emmerich am Rhein to destroy the bridges over the River Waal, the main distributary branch of the River Rhine, in Nijmegen in the Netherlands, which had already been captured by the Americans. The wreck of a *Biber* that had taken part in this attack was later discovered in the Rhine. It is now on display in the Rheinmuseum in Emmerich, together with photographic documentation. Although *Biber* submarines were in operation until April 1945, they were unable to achieve any further successes but suffered high losses.

Based on its design, a slightly larger version with the designation *Biber II* was to be developed. With a crew of two, it was to allow a change of watch and be able to dive deeper. This project did not make it past the planning stage. By the end of the war, a long-range boat, the *Biber III*, capable of traveling up to 1,000 nm was conceived. However, only a few towing models were built as parallel development named *Delphin* (dolphin) was more promising.

A *Biber* at the Technik Museen Speyer showing the position of the two attached torpedoes. (© Technik Museen Sinsheim Speyer)

Seehund

The previous midget submarines of the *Molch*, *Hecht*, and *Biber* types did not meet the operational requirements placed on them. These shortcomings applied to the manned torpedoes *Neger* (negro) and *Marder* (marten). However, all these vehicles were built under enormous time restraints and with increasingly limited resources. Nevertheless, they provided the Kriegsmarine design offices with important insights into the construction of more capable midget submarines. New boats were urgently needed for use in coastal waters threatened from the air and to combat enemy landing operations. The most successful concept, which went into series production during the war, was the two-man midget submarine *Seehund* (seal). Its basic design *XXVII B1* underwent several modifications until the OKM finally accepted the *XXVII B5* variant for further development. The first three prototypes built by the Howaldtswerke in Kiel were delivered to the Kriegsmarine in September 1944. In June, the OKM set a total production figure of 1,000 boats, but later reduced this to 600. During the final phase of the war, increasing Allied air raids caused a shortage of materials (primarily batteries), the partial collapse of the infrastructure, and thus delays in the delivery of parts. As a result, only 285 boats were completed by the time of the German surrender in May 1945, while a further 93 units remained unfinished at their production sites.

According to its specification, the *Seehund* was capable of surface and underwater navigation and could carry a G7 torpedo on each side of its hull. The displacement of the almost 38 ft (11.86 m) long single-hull boat with a 5 mm thick outer skin was around 17 tons. The design diving depth was 100 ft (30 m), but 230 ft (70 m) was also reached during operation.

While a 60 hp Büssing truck diesel engine served as surface propulsion and enabled a maximum speed of 7.7 kn (8.9 mph/14.2 kph), a 25 hp electric motor from AEG was used for underwater travel at 6 kn (6.9

A *Seehund* during the final stage of its assembly. There was one torpedo attached to each side. (BfZ)

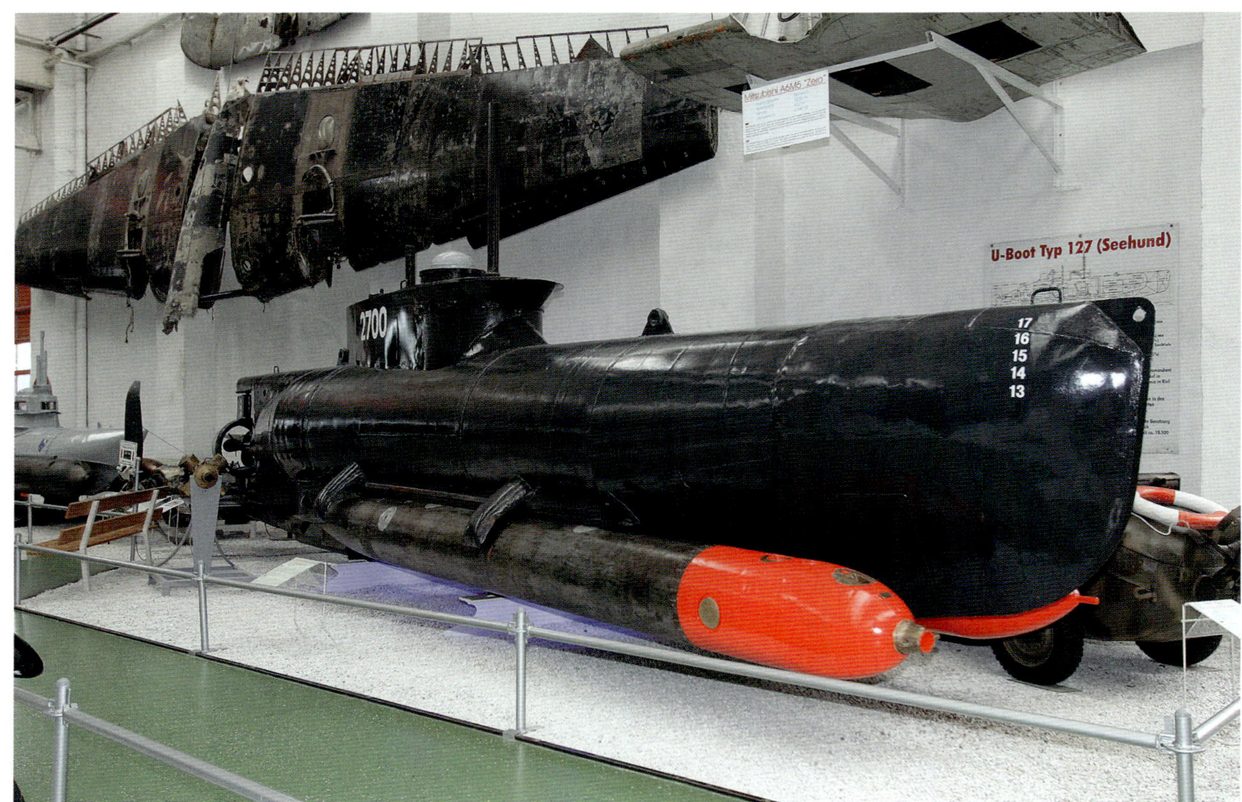

A preserved *Seehund* in the Technik Museen Speyer, Germany. A *Biber* is visible on the left. The museum is also home to a *Marder*. (© Technik Museen Sinsheim Speyer)

mph/11.1 kph). The maximum range of 270 nm (310 mi/500 km), which was possible with half a ton of diesel fuel when sailing above water, could be increased to 500 nm (575 mi/926 km) with additional external tanks. OKM had requested this extended range so that the *Seehund* could also carry out special missions along the British coast. The total of 36 batteries for the electric motor made it possible to travel submerged up to 63 nm (72 mi/117 km) at 3 kn (3.45 mph/5.6 kph) or 19 nm (22 mi/35 km) at 6 kn (6.9 mph/11.1 kph). To ensure that the boats could be used for several days, unlike the previous designs, the crewmembers had to take turns on watch. The food carried for these trips was as slag-free as possible, as there were no proper toilet facilities on board. Instead, a flat can with a large diameter was placed under the rear seat as a portable toilet.

Front view of a *Seehund* with its two torpedoes. The boat had a crew of two, whereas the *Biber* had just one. (© Technik Museen Sinsheim Speyer)

Design

The *Seehund* consisted of the flooded bow section with ballast tanks, the trim cell as well as the pressure hull. In the latter, the battery room with the compressed air cylinders as well as the control room and the propulsion compartment with diesel engine and electric motor were located. The commander/helmsman sat at the front of the control room and the engineer behind him. Above the commander's seat was the conning tower with windows and the access hatch (which was later made of plexiglass).

The boat had a 6.5 ft to 10 ft (2 m to 3 m) long periscope, a control stick for the rudder and diving planes, a course control system derived from aircraft construction, a listening device for detecting enemy ships, a radio, two compasses, two depth gauges, a snorkel for supplying oxygen to the diesel engine, an oxygen cylinder for longer diving operations, a manual bilge pump and the controls required for operation. Another diving cell (ballast tank), additional batteries and the fuel tank were located aft under the pressure hull. To be able to relieve the commander during an operation, the engineer had the same control system. While traveling on the surface, the batteries that powered the electric motor during underwater operation could be recharged, as the diesel worked as a dynamo by converting the revolutions of the drive shaft into electrical energy.

A *Seehund* lying on its side after being washed up on a beach without its two torpedoes. (National Archives of the Netherlands)

To attach the torpedoes to the *Seehund*, it had to be hoisted out of the water onto land or aboard a ship. (U.S. Navy)

Year/s of construction	1944
Builder/qty completed	ca. 7 shipyards/85
Length	38.91 ft (11.86 m)
Beam	5.51 ft (1.68 m)
Diesel engine	60 hp
Electric motor	25 hp
Propeller	1
Speed ↑	7.7 kn
Speed ↓	60 kn
Displacement	17 tons
Range ↑	270–500 nm at 7 kn
Range ↓	63 nm at 3 kn
Crew	2
Diving depth	230 ft (70 m)
Armament	2 torpedoes

Later *Seehund* versions were fitted with a ring-shaped, ducted propeller, also known as a Kort nozzle. This device improved the efficiency of the propeller as well as the turning circle, which was considered too large.

Seehund Operations

During its short deployment period of just a few months with the K-Flotillas 312, 313, and 314, the *Seehund* proved to be a highly effective weapon system. Thanks to its narrow silhouette and the quiet operation of its electric propulsion, it was difficult to locate by Allied detection systems. The boats were primarily used to disrupt enemy supply lines in the English Channel and in the German Bight (Deutsche Bucht). The operations lasted up to seven days, while the longest known mission lasted 11 days. The crew took the stimulant Pervitin (methamphetamine) to stay awake during the multiday voyages.

After Germany's surrender in 1945, the *Seehund* depicted here was handed over to France and renamed *S-622*. Today, it is on display at the National Naval Museum in Brest. (U.S. Navy)

A *Seehund* operating on the surface. It demonstrated good seaworthiness and maneuverability. (U.S. Navy)

The first *Seehund* mission was launched from IJmuiden in the Netherlands on December 31, 1944. It ended in disaster, as 16 of the 18 boats sank in a heavy storm, while only two returned. In February 1945, the first sinking of an enemy cargo ship took place on the east coast of England. On February 23, 1945, the French destroyer *La Combattante* sank after an explosion off the coast of Normandy. While British sources cited a mine as the cause, the Germans assumed that *Seehund U-5330* under the command of Leutnant zur See Klaus Sparbrodt had sunk the ship with two torpedoes. It later turned out that the ship torpedoed by Sparbrodt was the British cable layer *Alert*. The last missions took place on April 28 and May 2, 1945, to supply from the sea the German troops trapped in Dunkirk with food. Instead of torpedoes, the boats carried watertight containers. By May 1945, *Seehund* submarines had carried out 142 missions, during which they sank a tonnage of 93,000 GRT (depending on the source) or nine merchant vessels and damaging an additional three, while losing 35 boats, mostly attributed to bad weather. Around a third of the two-man crews were killed in action or taken prisoner. Several men also died from carbon monoxide poisoning due to the (initially) faulty engine ventilation. The fact that the *Seehund* submarines posed a danger to their opponents that should not be underestimated during the final months was demonstrated, among other things, by the fact that the Allies were forced to deploy considerable naval and air forces to fight them.

The *Seehund* could quickly descend to depths of up to 230 ft (70 m). Due to its low maximum speed of 7.7 kn (8.9 mph/14.2 kph), it could not pursue fast-moving ships. (U.S. Navy)

A Seehund *on a trailer ready to be transported to the coast. It was the first German midget submarine equipped with the technical systems of larger U-boats. (U.S. Navy)*

Too Late to Make a Difference

From the Allied point of view, the *Seehund*'s small size made it extremely difficult for *Asdic* (an early form of sonar) to get a return signal from its hull, while its very quiet, slow-speed running made it almost immune to detection by hydrophones. As Admiral Sir Charles Little, Commander-in-Chief, Portsmouth, put it, "Fortunately for us these damn things arrived too late in the war to do any damage," (Paul Kemp, *Midget Submarine of the Second World*, 2004).

After the war, the victorious powers took over several surviving boats for investigation and testing. France received four units and commissioned them as *S-621*, *S-622*, *S-623*, and *S-624*. They were used until August 1953. *S-622* (formerly *U-5622*) is now on display at the National Naval Museum in Brest. Other examples are preserved in other international museums and collections. Since the end of the war, several boats have been located and salvaged, some of which have been restored as museum exhibits. As the *Seehund* was far more successful in offensive operations than the smaller *Biber* and *Molch* types, some of which were built at the same time, plans were drawn up for further developments, but these never went into series production.

Delphin

The model towing tests and operational experience with the *Seehund* and *Biber* types made it clear that torpedoes attached externally to a submarine hull generated considerable resistance in contrast to freely towed torpedoes. This gave rise to the idea of developing a midget submarine based on a torpedo shape and thus capable of higher underwater speeds. This in turn led to the concept of a so-called "self-sacrificial weapon" (*Selbstopferwaffe*). Such weapons were already in use in various forms by the Japanese military in 1944: a boat loaded with explosives in a torpedo-like shape was to travel at high speed toward the target and destroy it by detonating the explosives on impact. The one- or two-man crew required to steer the boat were killed in the process. As this type of self-sacrifice was rather unthinkable in Europe, the design of such a boat, called the *Delphin* (dolphin), was eventually carried out without the idea of sacrificing its crew. The plans were the result of a collaboration between the Technical University of Berlin, the sheet metal-pressing company Ambi-Budd-Blechpresswerke in Berlin, and the development department of the command for small combat vehicles (Kommando für Kleinkampfmittel). The result was a technically not too complicated one-man midget submarine. Its production was modeled on automobile manufacturing in lightweight sheet metal-press construction. Like the operator of a *Neger*-manned torpedo, the pilot sat under a plexiglass canopy and used a stick for lateral and depth control. As the *Delphin* had no diving cells (ballast tanks); depth control was purely dynamic. The maximum diving depth of the 16 ft (5 m) long boat was around 100 ft (30 m). The propulsion unit came from a torpedo.

Since the *Delphin* was to be armed with an explosive charge and navigate toward its target when submerged, it was practically a submersible explosive boat.

The *Delphin* was to be produced at the Ambi-Budd sheet metal-pressing works according to the same mass-production principle as, for example, the VW Kübelwagen of the Wehrmacht shown here. (Bundesarchiv, N 1603 Bild-192/ Horst Grund/CC BY-SA 3.0)

The *Delphin* was designed in such a way that it traveled toward its target at a high speed of up to 18 kn (21 mph/33 kph). Shortly before impact, its pilot was to eject himself from the vehicle by operating a lever, while the boat was now to hit the target unmanned to detonate the 2,650 lb (1,200 kg) explosive charge placed in the bow. In addition to the possible use of explosives, attempts were also made to equip the boat with torpedoes and mines.

An Innovative Hull Design?

The *Delphin*'s hydrodynamic shape can be seen as an anticipation of the later USS *Albacore*'s (AGSS-569) hull design. This unique research submarine, built in 1953, pioneered the American version of the teardrop hull shape (sometimes referred to as the "Albacore hull") of modern submarines. Emphasizing underwater speed and maneuverability, the innovative design was derived from extensive hydrodynamic and wind-tunnel testing.

Due to the course of the war, the *Delphin* project, which began as late as 1944, did not make it beyond the testing phase. One of the three prototypes built suffered severe damage during a collision in January 1945. The other two were blown up near Lübeck shortly before the end of the war in May 1945 and all their documents were destroyed. A modified version with the designation *Delphin II*, which was to be armed with a torpedo or carry a mine in tow to the target, did not make it beyond the planning phase.

Year/s of construction	1944
Builder/qty completed	TH Berlin/Ambi-Budd-Werke/3 prototypes
Length	18.1 ft (5.5 m)
Beam	ca. 3.3 ft (1 m)
Electric motor	32 hp
Propeller	1
Speed ↑	10
Speed ↓	18
Displacement	ca. 2.6 tons
Range	Up to 300 nm
Crew	1
Diving depth	100 ft (30 m)
Armament	Explosives in the bow section

Unrealized Midget Submarine Projects

Type XXVII F

In the summer of 1944, the *Type XXVII F* midget submarine with a Walter turbine system was designed partly based on the successful *Seehund*. This propulsion system, developed by engineer Hellmuth Walter, was intended to generate sufficient power for the electric motors for underwater operations, where diesel engines could not be used: as the rechargeable batteries (accumulators) used at the time were still quite weak, an attempt was made to use a catalyst to convert hydrogen peroxide into superheated steam, which was fed under pressure into the turbine to drive it and thus generate electricity for the electric motors. The *Type XXVII F* was to carry a torpedo in a bulge underneath the hull. As the Walter turbine with seawater injection intended for these boats was still far from being ready for series production at that time, further tests were eventually discontinued. However, a modified design, *XXVII F2*, fitted with a Walter turbine with freshwater injection briefly revived the project. After some promising model towing tests, however, this design was also not developed to series maturity (for reasons unknown today).

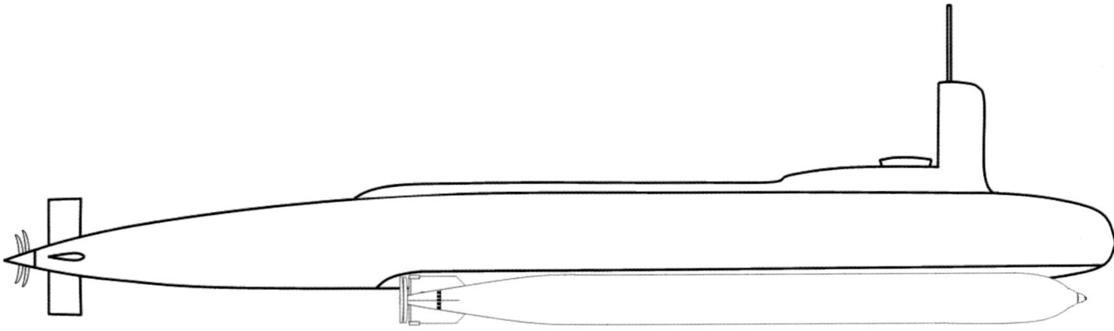

Simple drawing of the unrealized *Type XXVII F* midget submarine.

Type XXVII G

During the development of the *Seehund* (variants *XXVII B1* to *B5*), the Glückauf engineering office also drew up plans for the alternative *XXVII G* design in parallel. When the Kriegsmarine finally decided in favor of design *XXVII B5*, the Glückauf plans were unfinished, and the *XXVII G* project was discontinued. However, individual development components were incorporated into the final *Seehund* variant.

Type XXVII K

In mid-1944, the Germaniawerft shipyard began developing the *Type XXVII K*. This design was based on the *Hecht* and the *Seehund* but had apron-shaped extensions arranged to the side of the pressure hull, which housed the diving cells (ballast tanks) and the two G7 torpedoes. This gave the boat a hydrodynamically more favorable shape for achieving higher underwater speeds. In contrast to the *Seehund*, which only reached 6 kn (6.9 mph/11 kph) underwater, the *Type XXVII K* was to be capable of up to 11 kn (12.7 mph/20 kph) when submerged.

The engine was to be a new type of the so-called "circular drive" (*Kreislaufantrieb*). This was a method of propelling submarines independently of external air, known as air-independent propulsion (AIP). It consisted of a diesel engine that was to be operated underwater with compressed or liquid oxygen. The advantage of this system was a large operational range underwater at relatively high speed, as it was superior to driving with batteries, which were quickly exhausted.

Three modified and lengthened *Seehund* submarines, *U-5188*, *U-5189*, and *U-5190*, which were built at the Germania shipyard in Kiel and Schichau Werke in Elbing (present-day Elbląg, Poland), were to serve as prototypes. After the completion of the two boats in Kiel in early April 1945, the circular-drive engines also arrived, but these were destroyed in an Allied air raid before they could be installed. As the prototypes could not be completed by the end of the war, they were scrapped shortly afterward.

Year/s of construction	Not realized
Builder/qty completed	Germaniawerft Kiel/Schichau-Werke Elbing/3 prototypes
Length	45.6 ft (13.9 m)
Beam	5.58 ft (1.7 m)
Diesel engine	80–100 hp
Electric motor	8 hp
Propeller	1
Speed ↑	ca. 9.5 kn
Speed ↓	ca. 11 kn
Displacement	Unknown
Range ↑	Unknown
Range ↓	Unknown
Crew	2
Diving depth	Unknown
Armament	2 torpedoes

Type XXXII

In the fall of 1944, the Kriegsmarine's main office for warship construction (Hauptamt für Kriegsschiffbau: K-Amt) produced a plan study for the *Type XXXII* midget submarine. Based on the *Hecht*, it was designed for coastal operations in the English Channel.

This two-man boat, which was to be mass-produced, was to have either a purely electric or a diesel/electric propulsion based on the *Seehund* (depending on the source). Large U-boats and even very small submarines such as the *Seehund* were generally submersibles that traveled above water to reach their area of operation, dived for the attack, and returned home above water. This often made them easy targets during their surface voyage. *Type XXXII* was therefore mainly intended to operate underwater. For this purpose, it had to be able to lie on the seabed even when the current was flowing in the opposite direction, wait for the tide to change, and thus make the most effective use of the already limited range due to the low battery capacity.

As the two torpedoes were each mounted on the side of the conning tower, it was possible to reload them when the boat was in the water. This meant that no cranes were required for lifting it onto a pier or aboard a ship. The *Seehund*, on the other hand, had to be hoisted out of the water, as its torpedoes were mounted further down on both sides of the hull, thus making reloading in the water impossible, or at least very difficult. In early 1945, OKM ordered the discontinuation of all projects that had not yet reached the level of series production, meaning that the advanced *Type XXXII* midget submarine was discontinued.

Year/s of construction	Not realized
Builder/qty completed	Unknown
Length	38.9 ft (11.86 m)
Beam	5.51 ft (1.68 m)
Diesel engine	150 hp
Electric motor	25 hp
Propeller	1
Speed ↑	21 kn
Speed ↓	Unknown
Displacement	20 tons
Range ↑	80 nm
Range ↓	Unknown
Crew	2
Diving depth	Unknown
Armament	2 torpedoes

A larger 300-ton *Type XVII boat* (*Wk 202*). In addition to towing tests in water tanks, wind-tunnel tests with models were also used to develop the best possible shape for large and small submarines. (NHHC)

Type XXXIV

In the winter of 1944/45, the plan study for a fast midget submarine designated *Type XXXIV* for missions in and beyond coastal waters in the North Sea and Baltic Sea as well as in the English Channel was drawn up. The boat, with the smallest possible dimensions, was to operate almost completely underwater by using a snorkel and be able to achieve high underwater speeds of up to 22 kn (25 mph/41 kph) by means of the circular-drive system (*Kreislaufantrieb*).

The range was to be around 1,200 nm (1,381 mi/2,200 km) at a snorkeling speed of 11 kn (12.7 mph/20.3 kph). To reduce construction time and effort, the design was to be as simple as possible. A three-man crew was to be able to operate for seven days thanks to repeated watch changes. The *Type XXXIV* was to be armed with four G7 torpedoes, which were to be carried on rails in flooded chambers in the bow section. The 8.5 mm thick pressure hull was to consist of four sections that could be bolted together for easier maintenance and repair. Ultimately, the project was discontinued to utilize the dwindling resources for the midget submarine types already in series production.

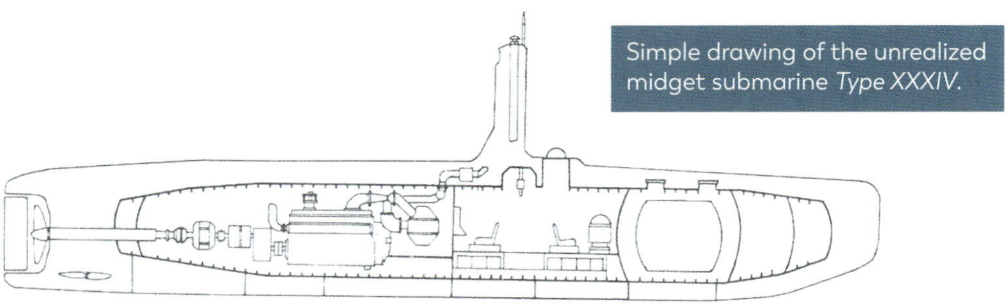

Simple drawing of the unrealized midget submarine *Type XXXIV*.

Year/s of construction	Not realized
Builder/qty completed	Unknown
Length	78.08 ft (23.80 m)
Beam	8.2 ft (2.50 m)
Diesel engine	1,500 hp
Electric motor	35 hp
Propeller	1
Speed ↑	Unknown
Speed ↓	22 kn
Displacement	9.8 tons ↑ /10.6 tons ↓
Range ↑	Unknown
Range ↓	90 nm (up to 1,200 nm with snorkel)
Crew	3
Diving depth	Unknown
Armament	4 torpedoes

Schwertwal

In the summer of 1944, under the direction of the K-Verband in Kiel (*Kleinkampfverbände der Kriegsmarine*, "small battle units"), an experimental model of a very fast underwater hunter-killer submarine called the *Schwertwal* (orca or killer whale) was developed. Although this idea had existed for some time, it was only the advanced maturity of the Walter propulsion system that made it possible to seriously pursue this project. Through various model tests in the wind tunnel of the Braunschweiger Luftfahrt-Forschungsanstalt (Aviation Research Institute), the *Schwertwal* prototype was given a hydrodynamic and torpedo-like shape to achieve the desired maximum underwater speed of 30 kn (34.5 mph/55.6 kph). It was to be deployed from mother ships.

The *Schwertwal* was equipped with an echo sounding device for the electro-acoustic measurement of water depths, an automatic course and depth control system, as well as an aircraft mother compass in a pressure-resistant container on the stern fin. It had no diving cells but was designed to dive purely dynamically by operating the diving planes. A control cell and two trim cells at the bow and stern were used for weight compensation. The primary armament of the two-man boat consisted of two innovative G7 torpedoes, which could be used to engage submerged targets with their advanced detection system. Although the prototype was completed, no more sea trials were carried out.

At the end of the war, it was sunk in Lake Plön in Northern Germany, but British search parties managed to locate and recover it in July 1945. After a brief investigation, the boat was scrapped in Kiel. Later calculations showed that the *Schwertwal* would probably not have been able to dive properly, as its shape and weight distribution had various weaknesses.

Simple drawing of the *Schwertwal.*

The *Schwertwal* prototype shortly before it was destroyed. (Former Kriegsmarine)

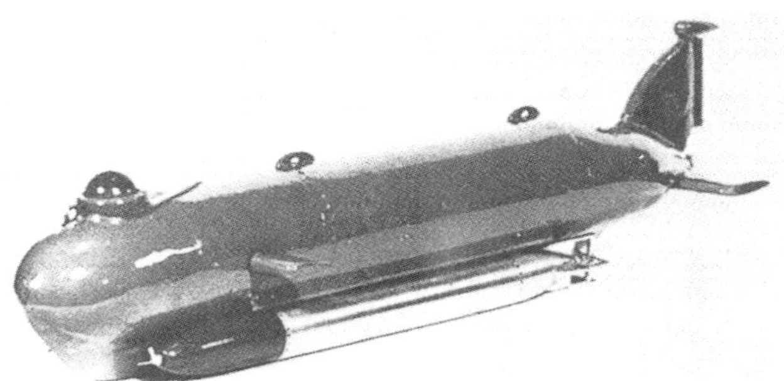

Scale model of the *Schwertwal* prototype showing details such as the rudder, the diving plane, and the attachment of the torpedoes. (Former Kriegsmarine)

The almost 300 ft (90 m) long pressure test chamber at the Flenderwerke Lübeck was used to test the integrity of submarine hulls through simulating the water pressure in various depths of water. (NHHC)

During its construction phase, a draft for a hydrodynamically better designed variant called *Schwertwal II* was created based on the experience gained in the interim, which was to have a special electric motor for operating slowly. However, this project did not progress beyond the planning stage.

Year/s of construction	1944–45
Builder/qty completed	Walter-Werk Kiel/1 prototype
Length	42.65 ft (13.0 m)
Beam	4.92 ft (1.5 m)
Walter engine	800 hp
Propeller	1
Speed ↑	Unknown
Speed ↓	ca. 30 kn
Displacement	Unknown
Range ↑	Up to 200 nm
Range ↓	2
Crew	ca. 330 ft (100 m)
Diving depth	S
Armament	1 torpedo

Manta

In the spring of 1945, Versuchskommando 456 of the small combat units began developing the *Manta* in cooperation with the Walther Werke in Kiel. It was a combination of a small submarine (for attacks) and an amphibious vehicle (for traveling to and from the deployment area). The vehicle was fitted with four wheels so that it could enter the water and return to land on practically any shallow shore without the need for port facilities. The displacement was 15 tons, the operational displacement about 50 tons.

Simple drawing of the *Manta*.

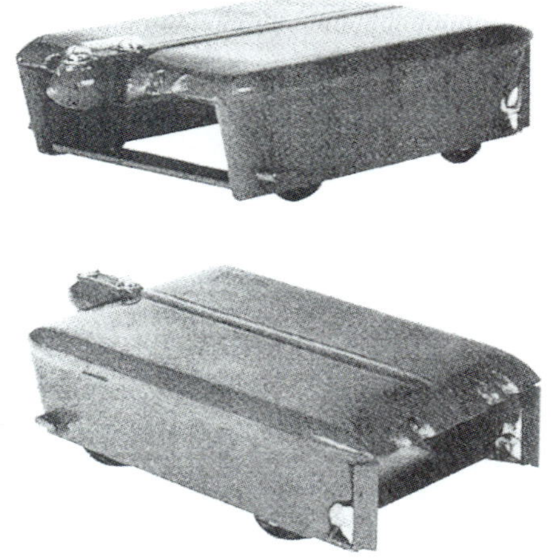

Scale model of the *Manta*, whose design was very unusual for a submarine. (Former Kriegsmarine)

The appearance of the *Manta* from the front was reminiscent of an upside-down "U". Some components, such as the pressure hull, came from the *Schwertwal*. The upper pressure hull served as the control center for the commander/helmsman and the engineer. The two side parts mounted on the outside and extending downward, on the other hand, were supposed to have come from the *Seeteufel* midget submarine (depending on the source) and housed the engines. By using existing components, the development time could be shortened. The armament should alternatively consist of four forward- or aft-running torpedoes, eight submarine-hunting torpedoes, eight to 12 sea mines or four missiles. To launch the latter, the *Manta* had to surface.

The maximum diving depth was to be about 200 ft (60 m). The propulsion for surface travel was to be a diesel engine (1,200 hp), while two Walter turbines with up to 1,000 hp each were to be used for submerged travel. The maximum speed underwater (never determined) is believed to have been between 20 kn and 30 kn (23 mph and 34 mph/37 kph and 56 kph) and even 50 kn (57.5 mph/93 kph) above water. The maximum range was to be around 1,180 nm (1,358 mi/2,185 km). As the project did not progress beyond the planning stage and all documents were (most likely) destroyed, the figures regarding speed and range circulated are often inaccurate and contradictory.

Year/s of construction	Not realized
Builder/qty completed	Carl Walther Werke Kiel
Length	49.2 ft (15 m)
Beam	19.69 ft (6 m)
Draft	Unknown
Diesel engine	1,200 hp
2 Walter engines	ca. 1,000 hp each
Propeller	2
Speed ↑	20 kn
Speed ↓	50 kn
Displacement	up to 50 tons
Range ↑	ca. 1,180 sm
Range ↓	Unknown
Crew	2
Diving depth	ca. 70 ft (21 m)
Armament	2 torpedoes or 4 mines; 1 machine gun or flame thrower for self-defense

Seeteufel

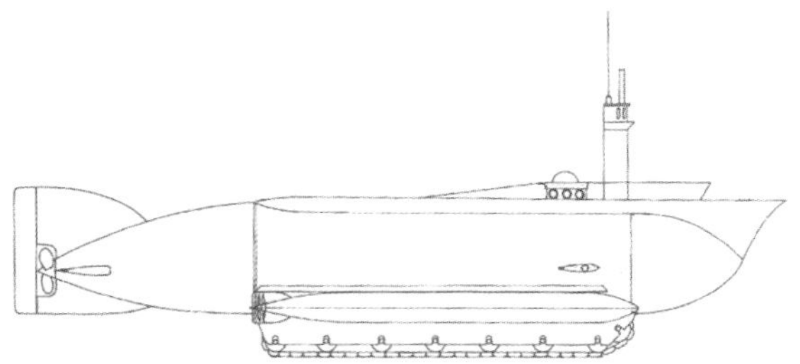

Simple drawing of the *Seeteufel*.

Stern view of the *Seeteufel*. Thanks to its tracks, it had amphibious capabilities. (Former Kriegsmarine)

The chain drive of a traction engine. The *Seeteufel* moved on land or on the seabed using the same principle. (Federal Archives, Image 101I-750–0001A-09A/Wolff, Paul Dr./ CC BY-SA 3.0)

Like the *Manta*, the *Seeteufel* (sea devil or anglerfish) was a midget submarine with amphibious capabilities. However, it had tracks on both sides (like a tank) that allowed it to roll into the water under its own power from an armored low-loader trailer. Thanks to its "offroad" capabilities, it could enter the water and return to land at practically any shallow shoreline without having to rely on crane ships, railroad or harbor cranes, or port facilities. This gave the vehicle a great deal of flexibility in its choice of location. It could also travel on the seabed or be set down on it.

The concept for the *Seeteufel* was the idea of engineer Alois Lödige. After the project's start in mid-1944, it took him and his team only four months to complete a prototype at the Eckernförde torpedo research institute. During sea trials in Eckernförde Bay, the vehicle lived up to expectations: it dived to the bottom of the 70 foot (21 m) deep bay and maneuvered very well. The pilot steered the *Seeteufel* using a control stick, which could be used to maneuver it in all directions like an airplane. The fast-responding diving plane allowed easy depth control as well as a dynamic descent and ascent. A wave-breaker made of plexiglass provided the driver with a good view. The primary armament consisted of two G7 torpedoes or four sea mines.

A machine gun or flamethrower was used for self-defense. Although the *Seeteufel* was to be equipped with a 200 hp diesel engine for surface travel and a 100 hp electric motor for underwater operation, it only received an 80 hp diesel engine and a 24 hp electric motor and was therefore underpowered. In addition, the tracks proved to be too narrow: the increased ground pressure caused the vehicle to sink deep into the mud or sand on shore, making it very slow or causing it to get stuck. Wider tracks were intended to reduce ground pressure and thus solve this problem. Finally, the *Seeteufel*, which weighed up to 20 tons, suffered from its weight, earning it the nickname "elephant." These problems were to be rectified before the start of the planned series production at the Borgwardwerke in Bremen. Of the 23 *Seeteufel* ordered, none were completed by the end of the war and the prototype was blown up in Lübeck. Although further variants were planned to include wire-guided torpedoes for combat diving operations, these were not realized.

Year/s of construction	1944
Builder/qty completed	Torpedoversuchsanstalt Eckernförde/1 prototype
Length	ca. 13.5 m
Beam	44.29 ft (2 m)
Diesel engine	80 hp
Electric motor	24 hp
Propeller	1
Speed ↑	10
Speed ↓	8
Displacement	20 tons
Range ↑	Unknown
Range ↓	Unknown
Crew	2
Diving depth	ca. 70 ft (21 m)
Armament	2 torpedoes or 4 mines; 1 machine gun or flamethrower for self-defense

Tarpon

In 1944, U-boat commander Fritz Kalipke had the idea of developing a midget submarine armed with two torpedoes that were not located underneath or to the side of the hull as in previous designs, but one below the other at the forecastle. In his opinion, this would mean that the submarine would be shorter and easier to handle for the driver on the long return trip after the torpedoes had been fired. To test this idea in practice, the Kriegsmarine's command of small combat units at the Kiel Howaldtswerke had a plan study drawn up for the *Tarpon* (tarpon fish) using components from the *Hecht*, among others. The midget submarine was to have an all-electric propulsion system that would give it a range of up to 180 nm (100 mi/333 km) with a displacement of 4 to 5 tons. The two torpedoes attached to the lower section of the bow were to be partly placed in tubes, with their openings closing automatically after firing. When the planning had progressed sufficiently that the construction of a prototype could begin, the war ended and with it all work on the *Tarpon* project.

Year/s of construction	Not realized
Builder/qty completed	Howaldswerke Kiel
Length	34.09 ft (10.39 m)
Beam	5.58 ft (1.7 m)
Draft	Unknown
Electric motor	13 hp
Propeller	1
Speed ↑	5.7 kn
Speed ↓	4 kn
Displacement	4–5 tons (or more)
Range	180 nm
Crew	2
Diving depth	130 ft (40 m)
Armament	2 torpedoes

Grundhai

The Kriegsmarine had no vessels or equipment to rescue damaged submarines and their crews from great depths; the only existing diving system from the Kiel-based company Hagenuk only worked down to a depth of 500 ft (150 m). As a result, the development of a deep-sea midget submarine began. The aptly named *Grundhai* (requiem shark) was to be able to reach depths of up to 3,300 ft (1,000 m) and was to have all the usual submarine systems, including control and trim cells. Three powerful searchlights were to facilitate the search for damaged U-boats on the seabed. As the *Grundhai* was designed purely for underwater travel, it was almost rectangular with only a slight rounding at the bow and a tapered stern, where a plexiglass canopy and the steering gear were located.

The propulsion system consisted of two electric motors, which also acted as a diving plane. They could be operated independently of each other to the left and right of the bow. Two tracks on four wheels enabled the *Grundhai* to maneuver on the seabed, move on land, and park on a ship's deck for transportation to the deployment area. Communication between the two-man crew and their mother ship was via a telephone cable or a UT device for Morse code. The latter enabled a type of acoustic underwater telephony in which sound was used as the transmission medium.

The *Grundhai* was equipped with a magnetic grapple arm as a tool for attaching lifting balloons to the sunken U-boat. The load-bearing capacity of such balloons was between 250 and 1,000 tons. To lift a 500-ton U-boat from the seabed, two 250-ton lifting balloons were required, which had to be attached to the bow and stern of the sunken U-boat. The 250-ton balloons had a diameter of 26 ft (8 m) and a height of 46 ft (14 m). A hose was connected to their upper end, which reached the anchored mother ship on the surface. Once the *Grundhai* had securely attached the balloons, the balloons would be filled with compressed air and ascend to the surface together with the sunken U-boat due to the resulting buoyancy. This technically demanding project did not make it past the planning stage due to the end of the war.

Year/s of construction	Not realized
Builder/qty completed	Unknown
Length	11.81 ft (3.60 m)
Beam	6.56 ft (2.0 m)
Electric motor	3 hp each
Propeller	2
Speed ↑	1.5 kn
Speed ↓	Unknown
Displacement	Unknown
Range	Unknown
Crew	1
Diving depth	3,280 ft (1,000 m)
Armament	-

K-Projekt

After the Japanese attack on Pearl Harbor on December 7, 1941, in which five midget submarines also took part, the OKM design office showed interest in a planning study for a similar submarine designated the *K-Projekt*. In 1942, plans were drawn up and a towing model was built and tested. The cylindrical hull, tapered at the stern, was to be armed with three torpedoes in the bow section. The boat was given a small conning tower with windows for better all-round visibility. However, when the Imperial Japanese Navy refused to hand over detailed design documents of its own midget submarines, it was in breach of the Tripartite Pact (Germany–Italy–Japan), in which the allies had pledged their mutual military and technical support. As a result, the *K-Projekt*, which had represented Germany's first step toward its own developments in the construction of midget submarines, was discontinued.

Year/s of construction	Not realized
Builder/qty completed	Unknown
Length	83.1 ft (25.33 m)
Beam	12.14 ft (2.7 m)
Electric motor	138 hp
Propeller	1
Speed ↑	8 kn
Speed ↓	4 kn
Displacement	97.75 tons ↑ / 112.6 tons ↓
Range ↑	Unknown
Range ↓	Unknown
Crew	2
Diving depth	Unknown
Armament	3 torpedoes

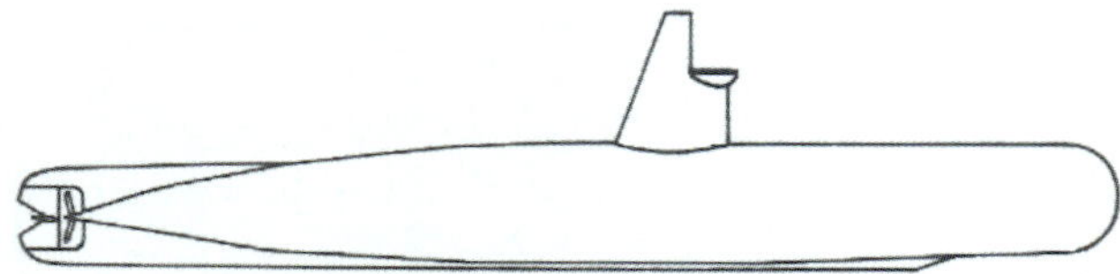

Simple drawing of the unrealized boat with the designation *K-Projekt*.

In Profile:
German Midget Submarines and Manned Torpedoes

Molch Midget Submarine

In the spring of 1944, the first midget submarine named *Molch* (newt) was developed for the Kriegsmarine based on the standard G7 torpedo. With a crew of one, it could dive to 200–230 ft (60–70 m) and had a top speed of 5 kn (5 mph/9.26 kph) underwater. Around 393 units were built during the war.

Seehund Midget Submarine

The most successful concept, which went into series production during the war, was the two-man *Seehund* (seal). Its basic design *XXVII B1* underwent several modifications until the OKM finally accepted the *XXVII B5* variant. Armed with two G7 torpedoes, its diving depth was 100 ft (30 m), but 230 ft (70 m) was also attainable. Its top speed underwater was 6 kn (6.9 mph/11.1 kph). In all, 285 boats were built by May 1945.

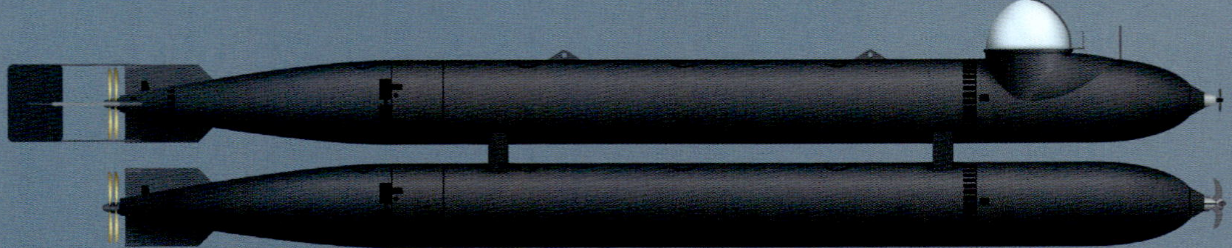

Neger Manned Torpedo

The *Neger* was the first German manned torpedo. Around 200 vehicles of this type were built during the war. The weapon consisted of two electrically powered G7 torpedoes arranged one above the other. Thanks to its small size, the *Neger* was difficult to detect by enemy sonar and radar locators.

Manned Torpedoes

Neger

Motivated by the manned torpedoes used by the British and Italians, the design of similar weapon systems began in Germany in 1943. In contrast to midget submarines, these could be produced more easily and in larger numbers if required. In addition, their small dimensions made it easier for them to penetrate enemy harbors or bays to torpedo enemy ships. They were to be deployed in immediate coastal waters, bays, and estuaries.

The Kriegsmarine's standard G7 torpedo, which was produced in large numbers and had proven itself in action, served as the basis. The development of the first manned torpedo with the designation *Neger* (negro), a so-called "one-man torpedo," was carried out by the Eckernförde torpedo research institute. The name goes back to the naval architect Richard Mohr as the "father" of this weapon: according to the usage of the time, the word *Neger* was derived from his name *Mohr* (black man). The weapon consisted of two electrically powered G7 torpedoes arranged one above the other. The upper torpedo contained a tiny cockpit with a plexiglass canopy. The pilot, equipped with a breathing apparatus and wrist compass, sat here.

The *Neger* was the first German manned torpedo. Around 200 vehicles of this type were built during World War II. (Former Kriegsmarine)

Year/s of construction	1944
Builder/qty completed	Several shipyards/ca. 200
Length	24.93 ft (7.6 m)
Beam	1.64 ft (0.5 m)
Electric motor	12 hp
Propeller	2
Speed ↑	4.2 kn
Displacement	2.7 tons
Crew	1
Diving depth	Not capable of diving
Armament	1 torpedo

A *Neger* shortly before being lowered into the water. The pilot put on an oxygen mask after the vehicle was put in the water. (Former Kriegsmarine)

The second torpedo (the actual weapon) was fitted with an explosive charge and mounted below the torpedo, which served as a vehicle. The torpedo was the only armament, as the driver had no weapons for self-defense. The aiming device consisted of simple iron sights inside and in front of the glass canopy. The driver then released the lower torpedo at a suitable distance of several hundred meters, which then ran toward the target on its own using its own electric drive. The driver then turned away to have a sufficient safety distance from the explosion in the event of a hit and to avoid detection. Thanks to its small size, the *Neger* was difficult to detect by enemy sonar and radar locators.

However, the manned torpedo already showed numerous weaknesses during its first sea trials. The biggest was its inability to dive. As the plexiglass canopy was above the waterline during the journey, it was clearly visible not only during the day but also at night, like a light buoy, as even the slightest night light refracted on the canopy. However, as the driver could not darken the plexiglass canopy as he would otherwise be disoriented, they tried to deceive their opponents with dummies: these consisted of a round plexiglass canopy with a weight underneath so that the canopy moved on the water surface in a way that was clearly visible to the enemy. A face was then painted on the canopy or its empty interior was fitted with a dummy head. As the *Neger* was not capable of diving, it was used almost exclusively at night to provide at least some camouflage.

The pilot sat under a plexiglass canopy. In higher waves, however, the canopy was often submerged, thus restricting all-round visibility severely. (U.S. Navy)

Neger Missions

The first combat operation took place in April 1944, when 37 units attacked Allied ships on the Italian west coast near Anzio. Due to adverse circumstances, none of the vessels involved was able to fire their torpedoes. When a *Neger* fell into enemy hands during the operation, the Allies were thus warned about this new weapon. During their dangerous missions, around 80 percent of all *Neger* crews lost their lives, mostly due to enemy defensive fire, technical problems, or suffocation. Today, some of the surviving *Negers* are on display in various international museums. In October 2024, the remains of a *Neger* torpedo were uncovered on a beach in Calvados, Normandy.

The design of the *Neger* and its torpedo attached underneath. (Former Kriegsmarine)

A *Neger* and its torpedo washed ashore after a failed mission. (U.S. Navy)

Operation *Overlord*

After the Allied landing in Normandy in northern France (Operation *Overlord*) in June 1944, manned torpedoes were used with some success against the invasion and supply fleet in the following two months of July and August. The *Neger* flotilla consisted of some 40 boats operating from the area of Honfleur on the southern bank of the Seine. On July 5/6, 1944, 24 *Negers* attacked the Allied invasion fleet, sinking two British minesweepers, HMS *Cato* and HMS *Magic*. Fifteen *Negers* did not return from the mission. Another attack with 21 boats took place on the night of July 7/8. These *Negers* were spotted in the moonlight and attacked by aircraft and ships. However, the Germans sank another minesweeper, HMS *Pylades*, and succeeded in irreparably damaging the Polish cruiser ORP *Dragon*, which was later scuttled. The sinking of the British destroyer HMS *Isis* was initially also attributed to a *Neger*, but later it became clear that the ship had hit a sea mine while at anchor in the Seine Bay. In addition, several smaller ships were destroyed or severely damaged by *Negers* and sea mines.

Marder

From spring 1944, the *Marder* (marten), a slightly larger successor to the flawed *Neger*, was built at the Eckernförde torpedo testing facility. The main difference was that the *Marder* had a diving cell in front of the driver's seat, allowing it to dive to a depth of 33 ft (10 m) (or deeper, depending on the source) for a short time. If visibility was good, the driver could also release the torpedo underwater so that it did not become a surface runner which could be seen by the enemy.

A preserved *Marder* with its torpedo in the Aalborg Maritime Museum, Denmark. Depending on the source, up to 300 units were built, some of which are still preserved in museums and collections. (© Springeren-Maritimt Oplevelsescenter, Denmark)

View into the *Marder* cockpit. (© Springeren-Maritimt Oplevelsescenter, Denmark)

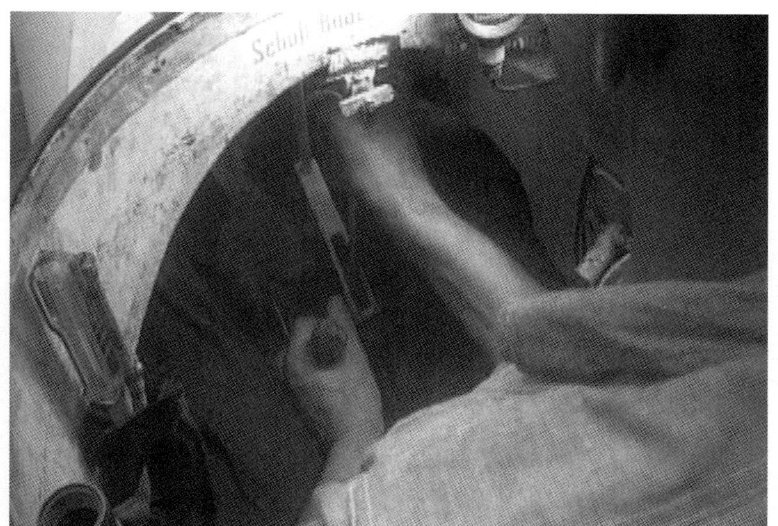

View into a *Marder* cockpit during World War II. (U.S. Navy)

Both the *Neger* and the *Marder* had the problem that the plexiglass canopy, which was just above the water surface, often became submerged even in light seas and the driver then had no forward visibility. Splash water and a possible oil film on the water also made him practically blind. If the driver then opened the hood, there was a risk that water would flow in and the vehicle would sink. The idea that many manned torpedoes of the *Neger* and *Marder* types could stop or at least weaken the Allied invasion fleets in the Mediterranean and later in Normandy sounded attractive, but the reality was different. The pilot often failed to reach his deployment area due to adverse weather conditions or technical problems. In addition, he often became the victim of aircraft attacks or machine-gun fire from enemy ships, as the *Marder* and *Neger* had no armor protection. While the former could at least attempt to dive away in time in an emergency, the latter was an easy victim due to its lack of diving capability.

The *Marders* saw their first combat missions in 1944 in the coastal waters off Sanremo during the Allied invasion of northern Italy but were unable to achieve any successes. On the night of August 2/3, 1944, 58 manned torpedoes attacked Allied ships near Courseulles-sur-Mer in Normandy and sank a freighter, a minesweeper, and the British destroyer HMS *Quorn*; they also damaged a cruiser and a freighter. However, only 17 units returned from this mission, while the others were destroyed in battle or lost in accidents.

The last *Marder* operation in Normandy took place on the night of August 16/17, 1944, when 42 operating units attacked Allied targets including the old French battleship *Courbet*, which had been beached intentionally by the Allies to serve as a block ship and was therefore a worthless target. While two *Marders* concentrated on the battleship, the remaining units were able to sink a large landing craft and another ship. Depending on the source, it may also have been *Negers* that carried out the fruitless attack on the *Courbet*. Of the 42 *Marders* deployed, 16 were lost, while the Allies succeeded in capturing one *Marder* after its driver was killed by machine-gun fire.

Unlike the *Neger*, the *Marder* could dive. The maximum depth was around 33 ft (10 m). (U.S. Navy)

A *Marder* on display in the United States after World War II. Several former German submarines including the large submarine *U-505* and smaller boats (including the *Seehund* and *Biber* types) had been captured during the war or shortly afterward. After their inspection by American naval engineers some of them became part of museum collections. (NHHC)

A *Marder* in the Technik Museeen Speyer, Germany. This variant has a modified conning tower (probably added after the war). (© Technik Museeen Sinsheim Speyer)

Closeup view of the *Marder*'s propulsion unit at the rear. The bottom torpedo is missing its propellers. (© Technik Museen Sinsheim Speyer)

At the beginning of September 1944, 30 *Marders* attacked Allied shipping off the French Riviera, but were unable to achieve any successes and lost 14 of their units. The remaining vehicles fell victim to an enemy air raid at their base in Vertimiglia in Liguria on the Italian-French border on September 10. Until the end of the war, it was only used sporadically in the Mediterranean, in the North Sea, and in Norwegian waters. The loss rate of the *Marder* was around 70 percent.

Year/s of construction	1944
Builder/qty completed	Several shipyards/up to 500
Length	27.23 ft (8.3 m)
Beam	1.64 ft (0.5 m)
Electric motor	12 hp
Propeller	2
Speed ↑	4.2 kn
Displacement	ca. 5 tons
Range	ca. 48 nm
Crew	1
Diving depth	ca. 33 ft (10 m)
Armament	1 torpedo

Hai

In the spring of 1945, the longer *Hai* (shark) was designed based on the *Marder*. It consisted of a bow and a stern section with two torpedo center sections in between. As with the *Neger* and *Marder*, a G7 torpedo was mounted under the hull. Due to further developments in the interim, the *Hai* had twice the battery capacity of its predecessor. This gave it a slightly higher speed of 5.6 kn (6.5 mph/10.4 kph) instead of 4 kn (6.4 mph/10.4 kph

instead of 4.6 mph/7.4 kph) and a larger cruising range of 90 nm (104 mi/167 km) instead of 48 nm (55 mi/89 km). It also had an additional diving plane for a quick and short dive without losing time flooding the ballast tank. Until the end of the war, however, only tests were carried out with the prototype. These showed that the *Hai* was not very seaworthy due to its excessive length. Moreover, it was difficult to maneuver. For this reason, it never entered series production. The prototype was destroyed at the end of the war so that it would not fall into Allied hands.

Due to its length of about 36 ft (11 m), the *Hai* proved to be too cumbersome and not very seaworthy. (U.S. Navy)

Year/s of construction	1945
Builder/qty completed	TVA Eckernförde/1 prototype
Length	ca. 36.09 ft (11 m)
Beam	1.64 ft (0.5 m)
Electric motor	17 hp
Propeller	2
Speed ↑	5.5 kn
Displacement	ca. 5.2 tons
Range	ca. 90 nm
Crew	1
Diving depth	k.A.
Armament	1 torpedo

2
Japan

To avoid another naval arms race like that before World War I, the leading naval powers signed the Washington Naval Agreement in 1922. This limited the size of the fleets of the individual nations, so that after exhaustive negotiations the strength ratio between the United States, the United Kingdom, Japan, France, and Italy was finally 5:5:3:1.75:1.75. This meant that Japan was only granted a fleet size equivalent to three-fifths of the American or British navies. With an allied Anglo-American naval force, this would have meant a hopeless power ratio of 10 to 3 against Japan.

To compensate for this numerical inferiority, the Japanese therefore concentrated on the development of high-quality and powerful warships in the following years and turned their attention to weapon systems which were not restricted by the treaty. These included submarines and various torpedo-carrying weapons. These two systems had always been favored by weaker navies to compensate for their material inferiority. One notable weapon that emerged was the Japanese *Long Lance* torpedo, which proved to be one of the most effective torpedoes of World War II. In addition to the construction of large submarines, the late 1920s also saw the development of various small naval weapons. In the event of war, these were intended to support carrier-based aircraft in attacks on ports and ships by operating in shallow waters close to the coast or by advancing to the berths of enemy naval forces.

After the end of World War II some 300 midget submarines of various types were found in various stockpiles in Japan. Fitted with 1,300 lb (590 kg) warheads to be used in self-sacrifice attacks, they were intended to ram enemy ships in the event of an Allied mainland invasion; however, there is no evidence that they were ever used.

As Japan had excellent torpedoes such as the *Type 93* (*Long Lance*) shown here, these weapons were not only to be used by aircraft or large submarines, but also by midget submarines in bays or enemy harbors. Some torpedo types also served as the basis for manned torpedoes such as the *Kaiten*, a self-sacrificial weapon. (U.S. Navy)

Midget Submarines

Little Fly (No. 1 and No. 2)

After Japan had succeeded in overcoming various technical difficulties in submarine construction by the early 1930s, the design of two prototypes began as the basis for future midget submarines. In 1934, these two units, numbered 1 and 2 (project name *Little Fly*), were completed at the Kure naval shipyard under the utmost secrecy. With a length of just under 79 ft (24 m) and a displacement of up to 46 tons, the torpedo-shaped boat had just a very low conning tower. Its 600 hp electric motor enabled a remarkable top speed of 24 kn (27.6 mph/44.5 kph) while submerged. The crew consisted of a commander and an engineer, and the armament included two 18 in (45 cm) torpedoes. After extensive sea trials, the findings were incorporated into the two test boats *Ha-1* and *Ha-2*. The fate of boats *No. 1* and *No. 2* is not known.

This photo (most likely) shows the *Little Fly* prototype built in 1934. It had a very small conning tower, while later boats were built with larger ones. (Former Imperial Japanese Navy)

Year/s of construction	1934
Builder/qty completed	Naval Shipyard Kure/2
Length	78.41 ft (23.90 m)
Beam	6.07 ft (1.85 m)
Electric motor	600 hp
Propeller	1
Speed ↑	Unknown
Speed ↓	24 kn
Displacement	46 tons
Range ↑	Unknown
Range ↓	Unknown
Crew	2
Diving depth	ca. 330 ft (100 m)
Armament	2 torpedoes

Type A Experimental Submarine Class

In 1936, two further prototypes (*Ha-1* and *Ha-2*) were built in Kure as the *Type A experimental submarine class* based on the experience gained from the first two boats. Although the basic design remained almost the same, the new boats were built with a larger conning tower, which, however, caused a slight loss of speed of 2 kn (2.3 mph/3.7 kph) when traveling on the surface. After sea trials, the Imperial Japanese Navy classified the two units as generally operational but decided against a series production and utilized the experience gained with *Ha-1* and *Ha-2* to develop the *Type A* to build that variant in series from 1938 on.

Drawing of a large *I-15*-class submarine from a U.S. Navy ship identification book. As the development of the *Type A experimental submarine class* had already revealed the short range of midget submarines, the idea of transporting them to the theater of operations on large submarines arose early on. (U.S. Navy)

Year/s of construction	1936
Builder/qty completed	Kure/2
Length	78.41 ft (23.90 m)
Beam	6.07 ft (1.85 m)
Electric motor	600 hp
Propeller	1
Speed ↑	Unknown
Speed ↓	ca. 22 kn
Displacement	46 tons
Range ↑	Unknown
Range ↓	Unknown
Crew	2
Diving depth	ca. 330 ft (100 m)
Armament	2 torpedoes

Type A

The series production boats of the *Type A ko-hyoteki ko-gata* (*Target A, Type A*) largely conformed with their predecessor. Their primary armament consisted of two *Type 97* 18 in (45 cm) torpedoes arranged one above the other in the bow. While the units completed before the outbreak of the Pacific War had free-floating torpedo tubes, the later versions were fitted with sealing caps to protect the two torpedoes from possible damage (collisions with other ships or underwater net barriers). The *Type A* boats were built in two shipyards in Kure. They were given the designations *Ha-3* to *Ha-52* and *Ha-54* to *Ha-61*. The number *Ha-53* was reserved for the planned successor. As the *Type A* only had a range of around 100 nm (115 mi/185 km), large fleet submarines (mother submarines) had to transport it piggyback to the deployment area.

The *Type A* midget submarine *Ha-8* was sunk by the U.S. Navy near Guadalcanal in the Pacific in 1943 and later raised. Today it is on display at the Submarine Museum in Groton, Connecticut. (Carol M. Highsmith/U.S. Library of Congress)

The fleet boats *I-16*, *I-18*, *I-20*, *I-22*, and *I-24* were converted for this purpose. In addition to large submarines, several modified seaplane tenders such as the *Chiyoda* were also used for transportation. Another shortcoming was the inability to recharge the batteries during deployment, meaning that this could only be carried out by an auxiliary ship or at a base. The hull consisted (from front to back) of the bow area with the two torpedoes and the two forward ballast tanks (cells), the forward battery room with another ballast tank, the control center with the control system, the aft battery room, and the propulsion room with the 600 hp electric motor.

Salvaging *Ha-8*, a Japanese *Type A* midget submarine, in Guadalcanal. (U.S. Navy)

The control section accommodated the commander and the engineer. A compass system and a periscope were used for navigation. The narrow interior with a diameter of just about 6 ft (1.8 m) offered the two crewmembers hardly any room to sit or stand. The mixture of battery exhaust fumes and their own body vapors made the air almost unbearable. The movable counterweight in the aft battery compartment was used to balance the boat after firing the torpedoes. A total of 50 *Type A* units were built.

Attack on Pearl Harbor

The Japanese attack on the American naval base at Pearl Harbor on the Hawaiian island of Oahu on December 7, 1941, was intended to destroy the U.S. Pacific fleet stationed there with one massive blow. The aim was to eliminate the United States as a potential threat to Japan's militant plans for conquest and expansion in Southeast Asia. In addition to six aircraft carriers and auxiliary vessels, Japanese *I*-class submarines transported a total of five *Type A* midget submarines to the Hawaiian coast. There they were released from their mounts a few hours before the actual attack to sneak into Pearl Harbor. Although they had never been used in combat and had some design flaws such as an unreliable battery and trim problems, they were considered very advanced for their time.

Each of the five midget submarines that participated in the Pearl Harbor attack had a crew of two. The nine men who died that day are immortalized in this painting. The only survivor, Kazuo Sakamaki, who became a prisoner of war, was not included. (NHHC)

The destroyer USS *Ward* (DD-139), photographed here in 1919, was on patrol in the early morning hours on December 7, 1941, when the Japanese midget submarine *Ha-20* tried to sneak into Pearl Harbor. (U.S. Navy)

The five midget submarines *Ha-16*, *Ha-18*, *Ha-19*, *Ha-20*, and *Ha-22* selected for the operation had hardly been tested before the attack on Pearl Harbor. This mission was also considered so risky that the five crews were advised to "settle their personal affairs" and write farewell letters to their families as a precaution. On the morning of December 7, 1941, the American destroyer USS *Ward* (DD-139) was on patrol when a report was received on board that the minelayer USS *Condor* had sighted a submerged object moving toward the entrance of Pearl Harbor at around 0342. The USS *Ward* rushed over but was unable to locate any enemy or unidentified submarine.

Less than three hours later, however, the destroyer's lookout spotted a half-submerged submarine conning tower that appeared to be following the transport ship USS *Antares* into the harbor. At the same moment, a PBY Catalina flying boat flew over the scene and dropped smoke-detection buoys, as the pilot believed he was looking at an American submarine that had lost its way.

The USS *Ward*'s commanding officer, Lieutenant William Outerbridge, was not deterred by this and gave the order to fire at 0645. The first shot missed its target, but the second 4 in (10.2 cm) shell penetrated the submarine's conning tower. The USS *Ward* had thus fired the first shots of the Pacific War. When the submarine disappeared from the surface in a few seconds, the destroyer then dropped depth charges over the site, where it had submerged. The pilot of the PBY had meanwhile realized his mistake and did the same. At 0652, Lieutenant Outerbridge radioed 14th Naval District headquarters that he had just attacked a submarine that had attempted to enter the harbor. However, this report was slow to be relayed and only reached the commander-in-chief of the Pacific Fleet, Admiral Husband E. Kimmel, when the air attack was imminent.

The crew of the American destroyer USS *Ward* succeeded in sinking a small Japanese submarine as it attempted to enter Pearl Harbor. (NHHC)

The USS *Ward*'s gun which fired the first shot was installed as a memorial at the Minnesota State Capitol in Saint Paul, Minnesota.

Ironically, the USS *Ward* was hit by a Japanese kamikaze aircraft exactly three years later, on December 7, 1944, in the Philippines. William Outerbridge, then commander of the destroyer USS *O'Brien* (DD-725), had to sink the crippled USS *Ward*, his former ship.

Confirming the First Shot of the Pacific War

In the following decades since December 7, 1941, controversy circulated as to whether the USS *Ward* had in fact sunk a Japanese submarine. However, in 2002, the Hawaii Undersea Research Laboratory (HURL) discovered the submarine sunk by the USS *Ward* on December 7, 1941. The wreck lies intact in 1,100 ft (335 m) of water just a few miles from where the USS *Ward*'s commanding officer reported the sinking. Subsequent investigations revealed that it was *Ha-20*.

Bow view of the wreck of *Ha-20*, which was sunk by the USS *Ward*. The torpedoes are still inside the two tubes. (© Hawaii Undersea Research Laboratory/HURL)

A single 4 in diameter hole in the hull, just below *Ha-20*'s conning tower, marks the first shot fired in the Pacific War. The two crewmembers were killed. (© HURL)

The Lost Midget Submarines of Pearl Harbor

In 2002, the Hawaii Undersea Research Laboratory (HURL) under the leadership of chief submersible pilot Terry Kerby discovered the wreck of the Japanese midget submarine *Ha-20* sunk by the USS *Ward* on December 7, 1941.

Resting in a depth of 1,100 ft (335 m) of water, it remains as in-situ physical evidence of one of the most significant events leading to America's entry into World War II. Since its discovery in 2002, *Ha-20* has become the focus of a management cooperation between National Oceanic and Atmospheric Administration's (NOAA's) Office of National Marine Sanctuaries, the Hawaii Undersea Research Laboratory (HURL), the National Park Service (NPS), and the Naval Historical Center (NHC). Preservation specialists are investigating various factors including the submarine's corrosion rate and are interested in developing management practices for deep-water maritime heritage sites such as shipwrecks. In December 2003, an exterior corrosion study was initiated during a combined visit of NOAA and the National Park Service to *Ha-20*. This study applied methods like those used on the wreck on the battleship USS *Arizona*, also sunk during the attack on Pearl Harbor.

In August of 2005, HURL's deep sea submersibles *Pisces IV* and *Pisces V* revisited the Japanese midget submarine. For two days, various experts from the Hawaii Undersea Research Lab, NOAA's Office of National Marine Sanctuaries, the National Park Service, and the Naval Historical Center surveyed the wreck to gather

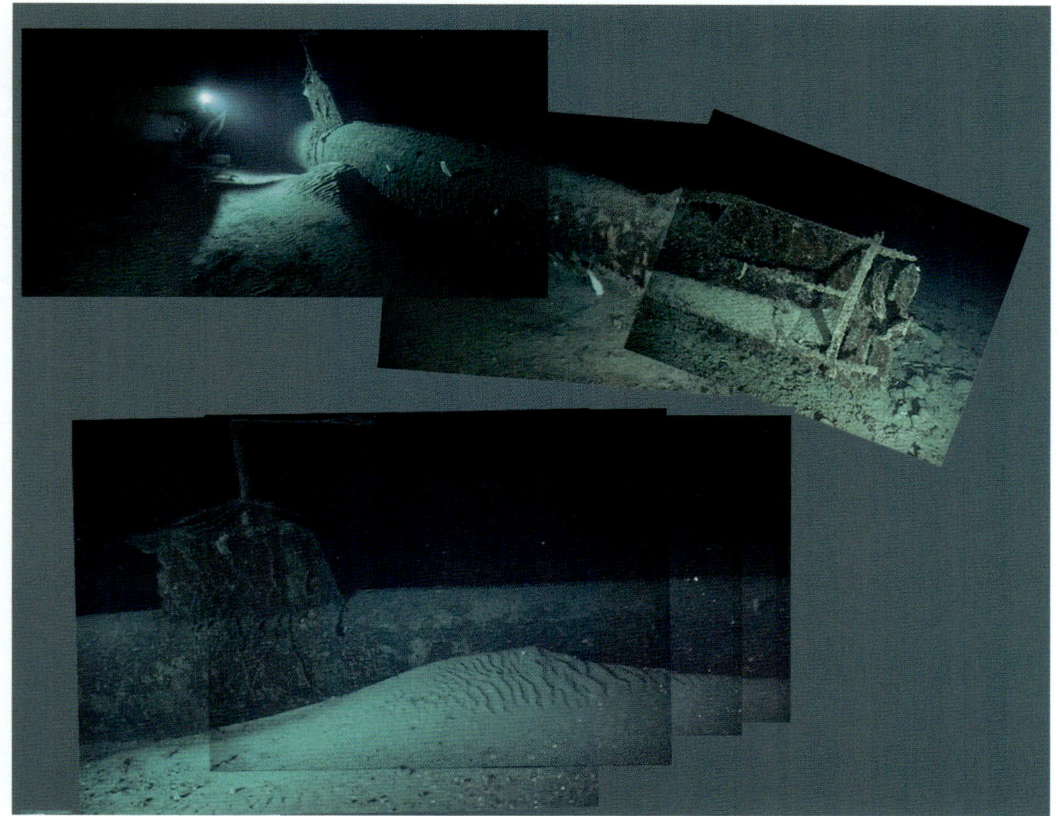

Side views of *Ha-20* as a mosaic image created from various individual photos. (© HURL)

View of the stern of *Ha-20* with its two propellers. This mosaic image consists of two individual photos. (© HURL)

baseline data for future preservation management. In addition, the scientists collected valuable digital imagery of the site to create a detailed photo mosaic of *Ha-20* and the seafloor scouring underneath its hull to be used for a stability assessment. Moreover, a camera endoscope system was constructed with the support of the Office of Naval Research to conduct a limited interior survey and assess the amount and weight of silt inside the wreck. The survey data gathered during the dives will be used to produce a finite element model (FEM) that will allow scientists to project site formation processes and discuss possible alternatives for preservation.

The wreck of *Ha-20* is a war grave as the remains of the two crewmembers are still inside. Moreover, it bears witness to the outbreak of the Pacific War on December 7, 1941. To enable future generations to remember, and to learn key elements of America's maritime heritage, it is the highest priority to minimize the impact of scientific preservation efforts to and treat the site with all due dignity and respect.

Midget Submarine *Ha-16*

In 1944, one of the other midget submarines that had participated in the Pearl Harbor attack was discovered in shallow waters off the entrance to Pearl Harbor and identified as *Ha-16*. It had been severely damaged by an internal explosive charge, which was probably set off by its two crewmembers when they realized that they could not escape. Their bodies were never found. After the U.S. Navy had raised the wreck, it was later secretly disposed of together with decommissioned war material in deep water off the harbor entrance. In 1992, under the leadership of its chief pilot Terry Kerby, HURL discovered the stern section of a Japanese midget submarine in 1,500 ft of water, which proved to be the first of three pieces of *Ha-16* found in 1944 and dumped shortly thereafter. Subsequently, HURL discovered the other two sections in 2000 and 2001.

Under an agreement with the Japanese government, midget submarines *Ha-16* and *Ha-20* are managed by NOAA through the Office of General Counsel and the Office of National Marine Sanctuaries' Maritime Heritage Program, as well as by the National Park Service.

Ha-20 is monitored to assess changes over time, particularly the ongoing corrosion. The submarine is protected by the Sunken Military Craft Act, which is administered by the U.S. Navy's Naval History and Heritage Command. (© HURL)

A Photograph with a Mystery?

On December 8, at 0041, the night after the attack on Pearl Harbor, Japanese forces received a radio message believed to be from the fifth midget submarine, *Ha-16*. It claimed to have damaged one or more of the large warships inside Pearl Harbor. At 0051 the Japanese received a second message that read "Unable to navigate." After that, *Ha-16* was never heard from again. In 1992, 2000, and 2001, the research submersibles operated by the Hawaii Undersea Research Laboratory (HURL) found the wreck of a midget sub lying in three sections three miles south of the entrance of Pearl Harbor. The wreck was in the debris field where much surplus American military equipment, including vehicles and landing craft, was dumped after the "West Loch Disaster," a maritime accident caused by explosions, which occurred just after 1500 on Sunday, May 21, 1944.

In 2009, a research team of various experts and HURL members including Terry Kerby was assembled by the PBS television series *NOVA*. During a series of dives to the wreck, they positively identified it as *Ha-16*, the last of the five midget submarines that had participated in the attack on Pearl Harbor. Its two crewmembers were Ensign Masaji Yokoyama and Petty Officer 2nd Class Sadamu Kamita.

As both torpedoes were missing, this indicated that the midget submarine may have fired them before sinking. This correlates with reports of a possible torpedo fired at the destroyer USS *Helm* (DD-388) at 0821 and two torpedoes fired at the light cruiser USS *St. Louis* (CL-49) at 1004 at the entrance of Pearl Harbor. However, there is dispute over this official chain of events. One "torpedo" seen by USS *St. Louis* was also reportedly a porpoising minesweeping float being towed by the destroyer USS *Boggs* (DD-136).

Some experts have intimated that circumstantial evidence supports a hypothesis that *Ha-16* was able to enter Pearl Harbor. There it fired its torpedoes at the large ships moored in Battleship Row and then escaped to the relatively quiet area of neighboring West Loch, where it was possibly scuttled by its crew. When accidental explosions sank and damaged several amphibious vessels moored in West Loch in 1944 (the "West Lock Disaster"), it is suggested that the sunken *Ha-16* was coincidentally found during the subsequent salvage operation and eventually dumped along with surplus military equipment.

A photograph taken from a Japanese aircraft during the Pearl Harbor attack shows what might have been *Ha-16* inside the harbor firing its torpedoes at the ships moored in Battleship Row.

The capsizing of the battleship USS *Oklahoma* (BB-37) and the sinking of the battleship USS *West Virginia* (BB-48) may have been accelerated by hits from submarine-launched torpedoes, which had larger warheads than the torpedoes dropped from Japanese aircraft.

Some experts suggest that the photograph shows sprays, where the paths of the torpedoes had supposedly started. These sprays could indicate a midget submarine rocking up and down due to the force of the torpedo launch. This movement could have caused the propellers at the stern of the submarine to become exposed, generating clouds of spray. One of the reports about the attack on Pearl Harbor confirmed the recovery of at least one unexploded torpedo identical to the ones carried by the midget submarines.

The possible fate of *Ha-16* and the theory that it was able to fire its torpedoes at the ships moored at Battleship Row and probably scored one or two hits is covered in the 2009 PBS *NOVA* documentary "Killer Subs in Pearl Harbor," produced by Lone Wolf Media. However, this theory is controversial and has been rejected by leading experts.

An aerial photograph, taken by a Japanese pilot during the attack on December 7, 1941, shows water movements and a torpedo trajectory that could have come from *Ha-16* (left). As the two torpedoes were missing, some experts believe that *Ha-16* could have fired them at the ships in the harbor. (U.S. Navy)

In 1992, 2000, and 2001, HURL's submersibles found the wreck of *Ha-16* lying in three parts three miles south of the Pearl Harbor entrance. (© HURL)

The mid-section of the captured *Ha-19* after the removal of its bow and stern for further studies by American submarine experts. (U.S. Navy)

The mid-section of *Ha-16*. All three sections of the submarine were dumped. (© HURL)

The intact conning tower of *Ha-16*. (© HURL)

In 2009, a research team assembled by the PBS television series *NOVA* positively identified the sub as being *Ha-16*, piloted by Ensign Masaji Yokoyama and Petty Officer 2nd Class Sadamu Kamita. Their bodies were never found. (© HURL)

Ha-16's damage was caused by an internal explosive charge, probably set off by its crew. (© HURL)

A *Pisces* submersible, operated by HURL, examining the front part of *Ha-16*'s mid-section. (© HURL)

Closeup view of the front part *Ha-16*'s mid-section. The cable was used to dump it in deep water off the harbor. (© HURL)

Ha-16's bow section. The two torpedoes are missing. Did the submarine fire them before sinking? (© HURL)

The bow section of the captured *Ha-19*. (U.S. Navy)

Closeup of *Ha-16*'s empty torpedo tubes. HURL's theory is that the submarine fired its torpedoes at the cruiser USS *St. Louis* (CA-49) as it exited the South Channel out of Pearl Harbor at 22 kn (25 mph/41 kph). Both torpedoes missed and one probably exploded on the reef. One dud torpedo was later found but it is unclear if it was fired from *Ha-16*. (© HURL)

Examination of *Ha-16*'s stern section. (© HURL)

The stern section as viewed from the front. (© HURL)

The stern section of the captured *Ha-19*. (U.S. Navy)

Side view of *Ha-16*'s stern section with its damaged rudder and propellers. (© HURL)

Ha-19 and *Ha-22*

The fate of the other four boats is also interesting: *Ha-19* was unable to reach the harbor entrance and ran aground on the east coast of Oahu. One of the two crewmembers, Ensign Kazuo Sakamaki, managed to swim ashore and became the first Japanese prisoner of war. The submarine is now on display at the National Museum of the Pacific War in Fredericksburg, Texas.

Ha-22, on the other hand, managed to enter the harbor and launch its two torpedoes at ships, but both missed their targets. At 0843, the destroyer USS *Monaghan* sank the submarine, which was later raised and used as filler material in the construction of a pier. In 1952, *Ha-22* resurfaced briefly when workers improving the pier construction at the submarine base hit the buried wreck with a dragline while excavating landfill. After digging a deeper trench, they rolled the wreck over and reburied it.

Midget submarine *Ha-19* that ran aground on the east coast of Oahu. Today it is on display at the National Museum of the Pacific War in Fredericksburg, Texas, also known as the Nimitz Museum. (NHHC)

Ha-19 after being moved onto the beach. (NHHC)

Bow view of *Ha-19*. The boat had ram protection for its torpedoes placed in the bow. (NHHC)

The sharp steel struts at the bow were also used to cut anti-submarine nets. (NHHC)

Ha-19's small control room with the helm. The boat was operated by two crewmembers. (NHHC)

Ha-19's interior after the removal of several components for further studies. (NHHC)

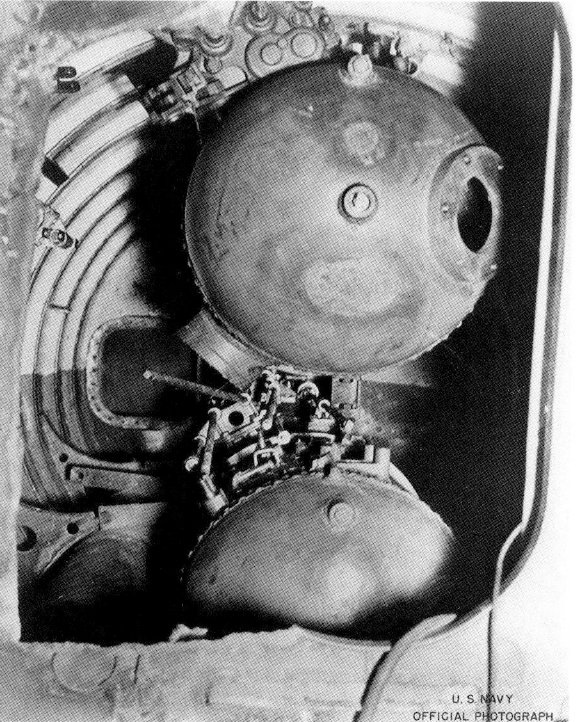

Closeup view of the two torpedo tubes in the bow section. (NHHC)

The captured *Ha-19* was sent on a tour through the United States to motivate the American people to buy war bonds, to help finance the war. (NHHC)

Wherever *Ha-19* was presented, it received a great deal of attention. (NHHC)

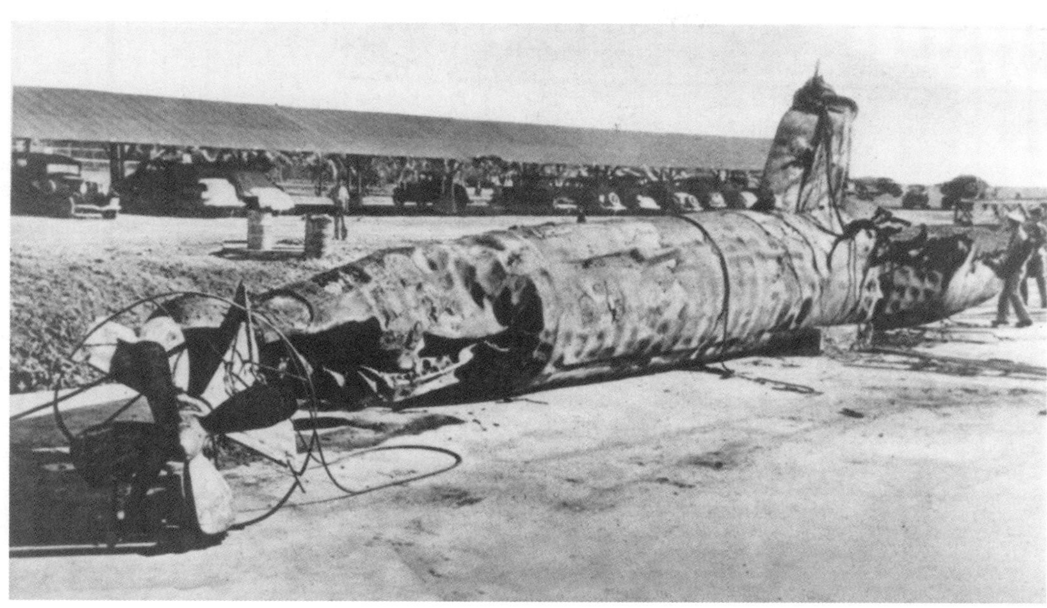

Ha-22, sunk by the destroyer USS *Monaghan* in Pearl Harbor, after being salvaged. The hull shows the damage caused by depth charges. The wreck was later used as filler material in the construction of a pier. (NHHC)

Ha-22's turret shows the hole from a shot fired by the destroyer USS *Monaghan* (DD-354). (NHHC)

Ha-18

In 1960, the wreck of *Ha-18* was discovered in Keehi Lagoon, east of the harbor entrance to Pearl Harbor. It was damaged by depth charges and no bodies were found inside. During the Japanese attack on December 7, 1941, several destroyers reported submarine contacts in this area and attacked them with depth charges. As a result, it is probable that a damaged *Ha-18* was abandoned by its crew, who may have survived, but most likely died after escaping their crippled and sinking midget submarine. As the wreck still carried its demolition charge and live torpedoes, the bow section (with the torpedoes) was unbolted, taken out to sea and dumped. At the request of the Japanese consul general in Hawaii, the submarine, without its bow, was returned to Japan in 1961.

The recovery of some artifacts, including a boot, a uniform, a glove, and tools confirmed that it was *Ha-18*. After restoration and adding a mockup bow, the midget submarine was placed in the grounds of the Naval Academy in Etajima in 1962.

Salvage of *Ha-18* from Keehi Lagoon east of the entrance to Pearl Harbor in 1960. The fate of the crew is unknown. (NHHC)

Further *Type A* Missions

Despite their unsuccessful attack on Pearl Harbor, Japanese *Type A* midget submarines were deployed on further missions. On May 30, 1942, two boats attacked British Royal Navy ships moored near Madagascar, sinking the tanker *British Loyalty* and severely damaging the old battleship HMS *Ramillies*. One of the submarines was sunk by depth charges during the defensive action, while the other was beached before sinking. Both crewmembers later died in a firefight with British soldiers.

On May 31, 1942, three Japanese midget submarines were to attack the American heavy cruiser USS *Chicago* off Sydney Bay in Australia, but the operation failed. As one boat was unable to fire its torpedoes, the crew scuttled it and then committed suicide. The second one became entangled in an anti-submarine net and its crew decided to blow it up (each boat had an explosive charge for self-destruction). The third boat, however, succeeded in firing its two torpedoes: one of these sank the depot ship HMAS *Kuttabul*, while the second landed on the shore. The boat itself was destroyed by depth charges. Shortly after the attack, both boats were salvaged. The components of both wrecks were later used to create one "complete" midget submarine, which is now on display in the Australian War Memorial Museum in Canberra.

In further missions, the *Type A* was unable to achieve any significant successes. This was due to the very effective American underwater detection technology and increasingly refined submarine-hunting techniques, but also to the fact that the midget submarines were less and less able to reach their areas of operation due to increasing American air and sea superiority. When the modified *Type B* went into series production from 1943, the remaining *Type A* units were gradually phased out to serve as training boats. Another *Type A* submarine (*Ha-8*) is preserved today in the Submarine Force Museum in Groton, Connecticut.

Japan's Alaskan Midget Submarine Base

When the United States entered World War II after the Japanese attack on Pearl Harbor, the entire garrison on small Kiska Island in the Aleutians consisted of just 10 men operating a U.S. Navy radio and weather station. In a diversionary attack as part of the Japanese attempt to take Midway, the Japanese invaded the Aleutians in early June 1942. Despite American naval and air assaults, they began fortifying the island and stationed 3,700 navy personnel at Kiska Harbor, as well as 3,500 army personnel at Gertrude Cove over the ensuing months. The harbor became the base for various types of floatplanes, fighters, bombers, and reconnaissance aircraft. The Japanese also built a slipway and repair facilities for midget submarines.

With a looming American force ready to invade the frozen tundra near the Bering Strait in July 1943, the Japanese withdrew their troops, scuttled their remaining midget submarines with demolition charges and blew up another one using torpedo warheads. The three partially cannibalized midget submarines in the maintenance shed were also demolished. The wrecks remain on the islands to this day. Kiska is federally owned and part of the Alaska Maritime National Wildlife Refuge, which is mainly administered by the U.S. Fish and Wildlife Service (USFWS).

The midget submarines after their demolition on Kiska Island. The one in the front is visible to this day. (U.S. Navy)

The wreck of the midget submarine in the front in its current state. (© Paul Jones)

Closeup view of the midget submarine's widely intact conning tower. Due to the explosion, part of the steel of the hull is bent upward. (U.S. Fish and Wildlife Service)

The widely intact starboard side of the hull with the two propellers at the stern. (Lisa Hupp/ USFWS)

Aft port view of the midget submarine showing extensive damage from shrapnel or firearms in addition to the damage caused by the explosives to demolish it. (Lisa Hupp/USFWS)

In Profile:
Japanese Midget Submarines and Manned Torpedoes

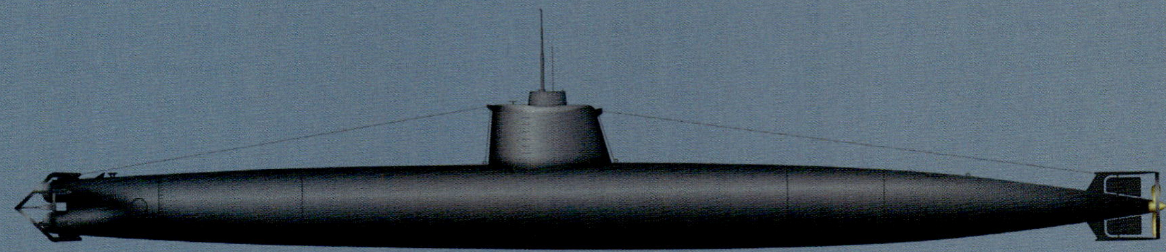

Type A Midget Submarine

The primary armament of the Type *A ko-Hotei ko-gata* (*Target A, Type A*) consisted of two *Type 97* 18 in (45 cm) torpedoes arranged one above the other in the bow. The *Type A* boats were built in two shipyards in Kure. They were given the designations *Ha-3* to *Ha-52* and *Ha-54* to *Ha-61*. (*Ha-53* was reserved for the planned successor). As the *Type A* only had a range of around 100 nm (115 mi/185 km), large fleet submarines (mother submarines) had to transport it via piggyback to the deployment area.

Kaiten Manned Torpedo

The *Kaiten* (change of the sky) was based on the *Type 93* torpedo. With 3,417 lb (1,550 kg) of explosives in the front section, the *Kaiten 1* had a significant destructive force. The pilots, partly recruited from volunteers for the air force's kamikaze (self-sacrificial) missions, who were retrained on the *Kaiten* due to a lack of available aircraft, were between 17 and 28 years old. By the end of the war, 1,375 personnel had been trained as *Kaiten* pilots. Their most successful attack occurred about 250 miles northeast of Cape Engaño off the island of Luzon in the Philippines, on July 24, 1945, when the destroyer escort USS *Underhill* (DE-682) was sunk by *Kaitens*.

Type B

1942 saw the completion of the test boat for the *Type B ko-hyoteki otsu-gata* (*Type B* class), which was to replace the *Type A* and compensate for its weaknesses in design. It had become apparent that the first generation of these boats often had to be transported to the deployment area by large submarines due to their insufficient range. Another major problem was the inability to recharge the batteries during deployment. The *Type B* prototype with the designation *Ha-53* therefore had a 40 hp diesel engine with a range of 350 nm (400 mi/650 km) in addition to the electric motor for underwater travel, which enabled a range of 120 nm (138 mi/222 km) at 18.5 kn (21.3 mph/34 kph). When the batteries of the electric motor were exhausted, the diesel could recharge them in about 18 hours during surface travel. Another difference to its predecessor was a third crewmember so that the crew could take over from each other on longer journeys.

The additional diesel engine also required more effort to operate than the electric motor alone. The armament of two torpedoes in the bow remained the same. The experience gained through sea trials was incorporated directly into series production of the subsequent *Type C*. The fate of *Ha-53*, the only *Type B* boat completed, is not known. Depending on the source, some *Type A* boats are said to have been converted into *Type B* boats and used for testing.

When the batteries of the electric motor were exhausted, the *Type A* boats had to surface, thus becoming an easy target. The development of the *Type B* with additional diesel propulsion was intended to enable a greater range on the surface while simultaneously recharging the batteries. (U.S. Navy)

Year/s of construction	1942
Builder/qty completed	Ourazaki, Kure/1 experimental boat
Length	81.69 ft (24.90 m)
Beam	6.17 ft (1.88 m)
Diesel engine	40 hp
Electric motor	600 hp
Propeller	2
Speed ↑	6.5 kn
Speed ↓	18.5 kn
Displacement	49.75 tons
Range ↑	ca. 350 nm
Range ↓	120 nm at 4 kn
Crew	3
Diving depth	ca. 330 ft (100 m)
Armament	2 torpedoes

Type C

In 1943, the only slightly modified *Type C ko-hyo- teki hei-gata* (*Target A*, *Type C*) was built based on the *Type B* test boat (*Ha-53*) and the experience gained with it. With the same armament, its range above water was 350 nm (403 mi/648) at 6.5 kn (7.5 mph/12 kph) and 120 nm (138 mi/222 km) at 4 kn (4.6 mph/7.4 kph) underwater. A specially constructed transport ship was used to deliver the boats to distant areas of operation. This mother ship could place the submarines in the water via rails. A total of 47 *Type C* units were built. After its conversion, one unit served as a minelayer with the designation *M-Kanamono*. The missions of *Type C* boats included defense against the American invasion fleets at Iwo Jima and Okinawa in 1945. The success of their operations and any sinkings of enemy ships are unavailable from Japanese sources due to the chaotic circumstances during the final stage of the war and have not been confirmed by American authorities.

Due to their short range, midget submarines were often transported to the deployment area by mother ships or large submarines. Once there, the boats could be lowered into the water using sliding rails. However, Allied air and naval supremacy made this plan risky. The boats were intended to attack the American island bases in the Pacific, which were spread out over a wide area, and to protect their own bases from the enemy. (Former Imperial Japanese Navy)

Year/s of construction	1942
Builder/qty completed	Ourazaki, Kure/47
Length	81.69 ft (24.90 m)
Beam	6.17 ft (1.88 m)
Diesel engine	40 hp
Electric motor	600 hp
Propeller	2
Speed ↑	6.5 kn
Speed ↓	18.5 kn
Displacement	49.75 tons
Range ↑	ca. 350 nm
Range ↓	120 nm at 4 kn
Crew	3
Diving depth	ca. 330 ft (100 m)
Armament	2 torpedoes

The *Type C* boat *Ha-62–76* ran aground off Guam in the Pacific in 1944. The crew surrendered three days later. After an investigation by the U.S. Navy, the boat was eventually put on display at the War in the Pacific National Historical Park on Guam. (Daderot)

Type D (Koryu)

The *Type D ko-hyoteki tei-gata* (*Target A, Type D*), designed from 1944 onward, was a combination of the predecessors *Type B* and *Type C*. Another name was *Koryu* (water dragon or misunderstood genius). Although all the experience gained up to that point was incorporated into its design, it had weaknesses as well. One of these was the battery charging time of 18 hours, which was considered too long. In addition, it was not capable of independent operations in the extended coastal area, so it had to be transported to the operational area on the open ocean. Since American aircraft carriers and submarines were already operating off the Japanese coast in 1945, transportation on surface ships to more remote sea areas or to contested islands was very risky.

The possibility of transportation on large submarines was limited, as Japan had already lost most of its submarines at that time and the remaining units were themselves hunting enemy naval forces. This meant that

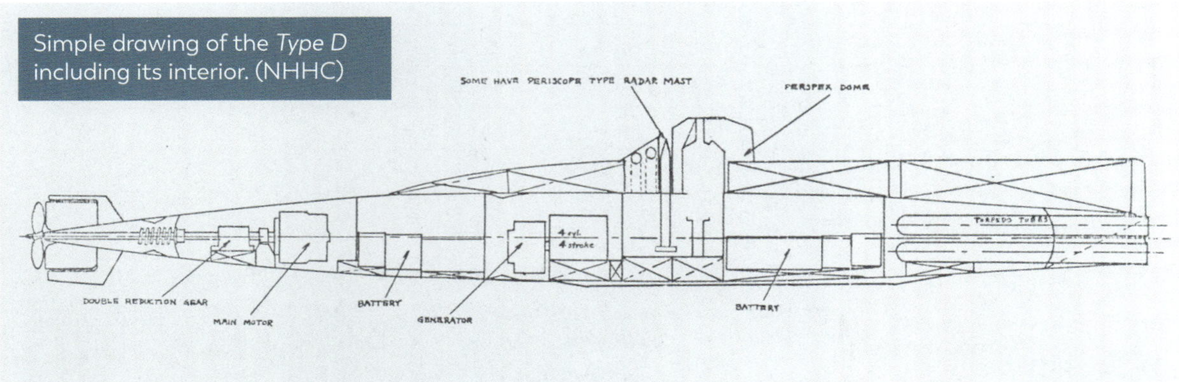

Simple drawing of the *Type D* including its interior. (NHHC)

The *Type D* was visually very different from its predecessors. Its hull was no longer cylindrical but had a stem above the two torpedo tubes to improve its seaworthiness while operating on the surface. (NHHC)

the main area of operation could only be the immediate coastal apron in Japanese waters. Nevertheless, the test boat *Ha-77*, completed in mid-1944, showed good results during its sea trials. It was also possible to reduce the battery charging time from 18 to eight hours by converting a 150 hp diesel engine.

The maximum diving depth was an impressive 330 ft (100 m). Overall, the displacement had increased from 50 tons (*Type C*) to just under 60 tons for the *Type D*—not least to have space on board for the five crewmembers on their multiday missions. Above water, the range was up to 1,000 nm (1,151 mi/1,852 km) at 8 kn (9.5 mph/15 kph) and 125 nm (144 mi/231.5 km) or more at 6 kn (6.9 mph/11 kph) when submerged. Even if 1,000 nm was a long distance, it must be considered that the boat alone needed several hundred nautical miles for its (very dangerous) surface voyage to the operational area beyond the coastal waters and back.

This meant that the actual radius of action was also limited to only a few hundred nautical miles. However, if the enemy had air and sea superiority, as was the case in 1945, the boat was forced to dive from its berth in search of targets. In this case, its radius of action was so small due to the weak batteries at the time that it was only possible to operate directly off its own coast. After the United States had conquered the strategically important islands of Iwo Jima and Okinawa, nothing stood in their way to attack the Japanese home islands directly. While Japan was thus preparing for an invasion by (primarily) American naval forces, small weapons such as suicide torpedoes, kamikaze (self-sacrifice) aircraft, and midget submarines were intended to repel or at least considerably slow the American invasion fleet in Japanese waters. Therefore, during the final phase of the Pacific War in 1945, the Japanese shipbuilding industry switched primarily to small naval combat equipment.

Incomplete *Type D* midget submarines at the Kure naval shipyard. These boats were built at 11 Japanese shipyards. The total construction time per unit was up to two months. (U.S. Navy)

After a few slight modifications, the *Type D* was finally ready for series production, but due to the dramatic deterioration in the situation from early 1945 onward, this could not commence until July 1945. About 570 *Type D* boats were to be delivered by September 1945, after which monthly production was to amount to 180 units. However, due to heavy air raids on Japanese industrial plants, shipyards, and infrastructure, only 115 boats were completed by the end of the war in August 1945, while about 500 more remained incomplete in the shipyards. Due to the lack of torpedoes, numerous *Type D* boats were to fight the enemy with warheads of up to 1,325 lb (600 kg) TNT. By the end of the war, none of the boats had seen any documented action. Whether the deployment of hundreds of units of this type could have stopped or delayed the enemy invasion fleet is speculative. Nonetheless, they could certainly have sunk or damaged several ships but with enormous losses of their own. No known boat of the *Type D* has survived.

The final assembly of the *Type D* was carried out using five prefabricated sections that were assembled. (NHHC)

The primary armament consisted of two 18 in (45 cm) torpedoes placed on top of each other with an explosive charge of 1,325 lb (600 kg) TNT each. (NHHC)

Year/s of construction	1945
Builder/qty completed	ca. 11 shipyards/115
Length	88.29 ft (26.91 m)
Beam	6.69 ft (2.04 m)
Diesel engine	150 hp
Electric motor	600 hp
Propeller	2
Speed ↑	8.0 kn
Speed ↓	18.5 kn
Displacement	59.3 t
Range ↑	1,000 nm at 8 kn
Range ↓	ca. 125 nm at 6 kn
Crew	Up to 5
Diving depth	ca. 330 ft (100 m)
Armament	2 torpedoes

Control center of the *Type D* with the helm and various devices. (NHHC)

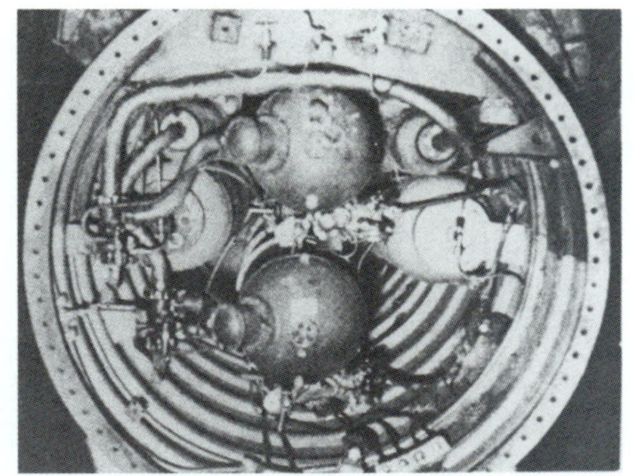

The bow section with the two torpedo tubes. (NHHC)

Kairyu

Parallel to the construction of the *Type D* (*Koryu*), the far smaller type *Kairyu* (sea dragon) with a displacement of 20 tons was built from early 1945 on. Its design was based on two test boats, one of which was a converted *Type A* midget submarine, while the other, under the designation *U-Kanamono*, was merely based on the *Type A*. In addition to the construction of the prototype, further test boats with different hull lengths were built to test different engine types. Eventually, an 85 hp Isuzu diesel engine was selected, which enabled a maximum speed of 7.5 kn (8.6 mph/14 kph) above water. For underwater travel, an 80 hp E-engine was used for a maximum speed of 10 kn (11.5 mph/18.5 kph). The above-water cruising range was 450 nm (218 mi/833 km) at 5 kn (5.75 mph/9.3 kph) and 36 nm (41.4 mi/66.7 km) at 3 kn (3.5 mph/5.6 kph) when submerged.

A *Kairyu* on display at the Japanese naval base in Yokosuka near Tokyo after the war. (NHHC)

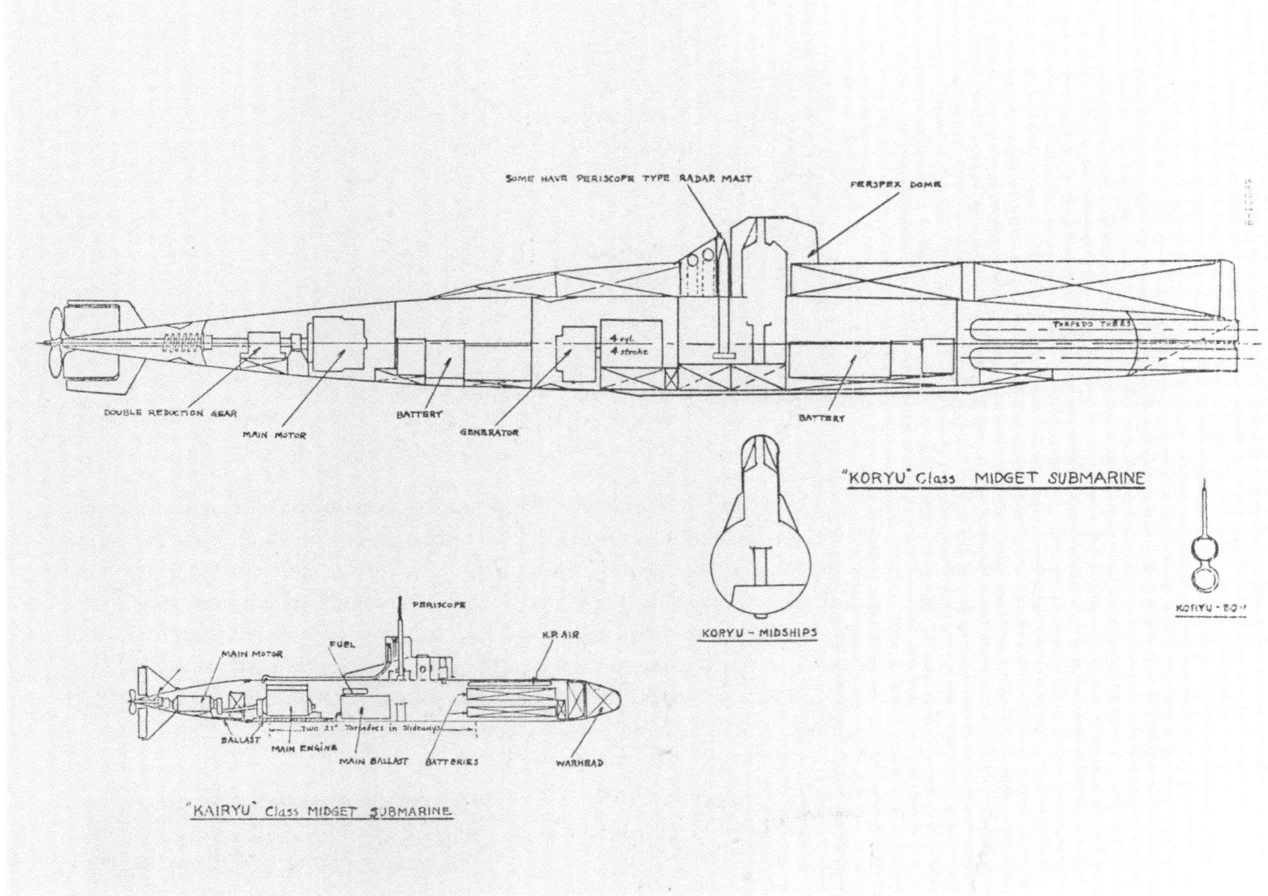

Simple drawing of the *Kairyu* including its interior. (NHHC)

While the larger *Type D* (*Koryu*) was intended to operate on the open sea to hunt down enemy ships, the *Kairyu* type was considered suitable for direct coastal defense in the event of an invasion. For this purpose, most of the boats were to be stationed off the strategically important waters of Tokyo Bay.

The diving depth was limited to 330 ft (100 m) due to the limited pressure resistance of the two 18 in (45 cm) torpedoes. Without them, the boat could descend to 475 ft (145 m). The *Kairyu* was given such a high priority in national defense that the Japanese Navy assigned it all material from canceled destroyer escorts. Construction was carried out from three prefabricated parts and took one month. Due to the shortage of torpedoes, numerous boats with a TNT warhead weighing up to 1,323 lb (600 kg) were to be used as self-sacrificial weapons. The plan envisaged the production of 760 boats at 11 shipyards by September 1945, but due to heavy air raids on the shipyards, only 213 units were completed by the end of the war, while a further 201 were nearing completion. The *Kairyu* type never saw action, with only 20 boats used as training units. One surviving example is now on display in the Kure Maritime Museum, also known as the Yamato Museum.

The *Kairyu* displaced only 20 tons and had a maximum diving depth of 475 ft or 145 m (without torpedoes).

View of the mid-section of a *Kairyu* captured by the United States. (NHHC)

A *Kairyu* midget submarine during trials by the U.S. Navy shortly after the end of the Pacific War in 1945. (NHHC)

Year/s of construction	1945
Builder/qty completed	Several shipyards/213
Length	56.69 ft (17.28 m)
Beam	4.76 ft (1.45 m)
Diesel engine	85 hp
Electric motor	80 hp
Propeller	1
Speed ↑	7.5 kn
Speed ↓	10.0 kn
Displacement	19.25 tons
Range ↑	ca. 450 nm at 5 kn
Range ↓	ca. 38 kn at 3 kn
Crew	2
Diving depth	ca. 330 ft (100 m) (475 ft or 145 m without torpedoes)
Armament	2 torpedoes or explosives

Kanamono

In late 1944, three more small submarine types, *Kanamono*, *Maru-Se*, and *Shinkai*, were built, all of which were regarded as emergency solutions. One of these was the two-man boat *Kanamono*. Its very simple design consisted of a long cylindrical middle section and a conical bow and stern. It could not fully submerge but merely undercut the water surface. A torpedo propulsion system enabled a maximum speed of 3 kn (3.5 mph/5.6 kph). The boat did not have a periscope, but only viewing slits in a small round conning tower. The primary armament consisted of an 18 in (45 cm) torpedo in the bow. Of the 14 boats completed at the Kure naval shipyard by the end of the war, none saw action. The fate of the boats is unknown; they were probably scrapped or scuttled.

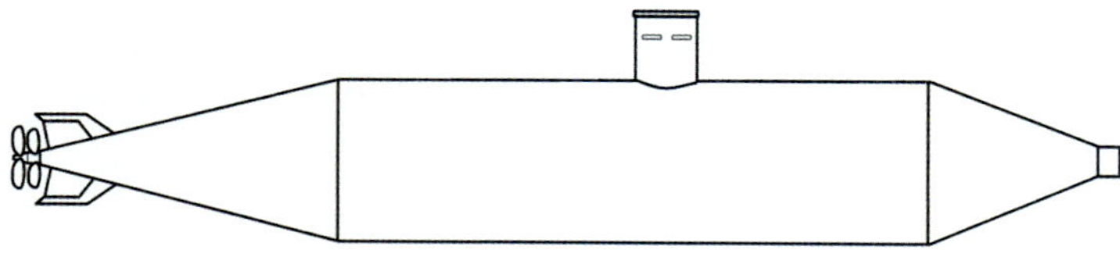

Simple drawing of the *Kanamono* type, of which only 14 boats were built.

Year/s of construction	1944–45
Builder/qty completed	Naval Shipyard Kure/14
Length	45.93 ft (14.0 m)
Beam	6.56 ft (2.0 m)
Diesel engine	Unknown
Electric motor	2
Propeller	3 kn
Speed ↑	15 tons
Speed ↓	Unknown
Displacement	Unknown
Range ↑	Unknown
Range ↓	Not capable of diving
Crew	1 torpedo
Armament	1 torpedo or explosives

Maru-Se

During the final phase of the Pacific War, the *Maru-Se* midget submarine was designed at the Yokohama Naval Shipyard in the strictest secrecy. No information is available about its appearance or dimensions. The propulsion was based on hydrogen peroxide, among other things. The armament was to consist of two 18 in (45 cm) torpedoes in the bow. However, the only boat ever built was scrapped before it was completed.

Shinkai

Shortly before the end of the war, Japanese desperation at the prospect of the imminent arrival of the Allied invasion fleet was also reflected in the design of a torpedo-like midget submarine type for self-sacrifice with the designation *Shinkai* (shaking sea). It carried a 2,200 lb (1,000 kg) explosive charge in the bow, which was to be detonated by an impact fuse when it hit an enemy ship. By the end of the war, only one prototype had been completed, but it was difficult to steer. In addition, it only reached 9 kn (10.4/16.7 kph) with its 20 hp electric motor. In theory, therefore, it could only have approached anchored or slow-moving supply or landing ships, as most vessels were significantly faster than 9 kn. For this reason, the project was discontinued and the boat scrapped.

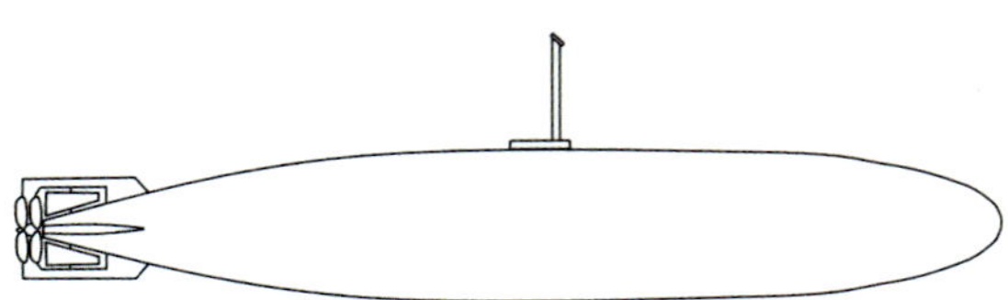

The *Shinkai* type did not make it past the experimental stage.

Year/s of construction	1944–45
Builder/qty completed	Naval Shipyard Kure/14
Length	45.93 ft (14.0 m)
Beam	6.56 ft (2.0 m)
Diesel engine	Unknown
Electric motor	2
Propeller	3 kn
Speed ↑	15 tons
Speed ↓	Unknown
Displacement	Unknown
Range ↑	Unknown
Range ↓	Unknown
Crew	1 torpedo
Diving depth	ca. 330 ft (100 m) (475 ft or 145 m without torpedoes)
Armament	Explosives

Manned *Torpedoes*

Kaiten

In the early phase of the Pacific War, when the Imperial Japanese Navy was gaining its first operational experience with small submarines, the idea arose of designing a vehicle called the *Kaiten* (change of the sky) based on the *Type 93* torpedo that would combine the advantages of boats (mobility and good protection against detection devices) with the speed and destructive power of the torpedo.

Despite plans being drawn up, Japan's naval leadership rejected the development and use of such a manned torpedo. However, when the military situation deteriorated significantly from 1943/44 onward, the construction of a prototype was finally carried out. To give the pilot the slightest chance of survival during the supposed self-sacrifice mission, the vehicle was fitted with an escape hatch. The majority of the future *Kaiten* drivers were recruited from the self-sacrificial units of Japanese aircraft pilots.

A preserved *Kaiten 4* in the USS *Bowfin* Submarine Museum in Pearl Harbor, Hawaii. The vehicle functioned practically like a submarine but served as a self-sacrificial weapon to ram target ships and destroy them by exploding its bow warhead. (© J. Messerly/CC BY-SA 3.0)

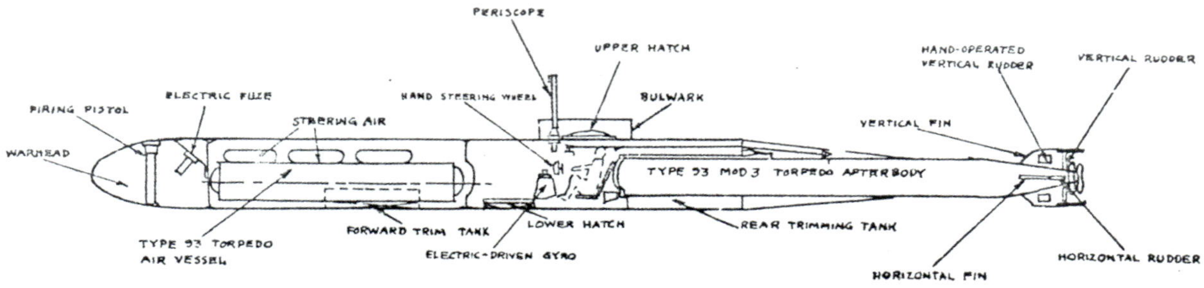

Drawing of the cylindrical *Kaiten 1*. The driver sat directly behind the explosive charge. (NHHC)

Kaiten Crews

Kaiten pilots were partly recruited from volunteers for the air force's kamikaze (self-sacrificial) missions, who were retrained on the *Kaiten* due to a lack of available aircraft. The demands were significantly higher than for the crews of the *Shin'yō*-class self-sacrificial boats, for example, as the *Kaiten* pilots had to deal with minor technical defects during the mission while remaining in the small hull for long periods without outside visibility. As the handling was quite demanding due to various weaknesses and therefore placed high physical and psychological stress on the pilots, many applicants failed the qualification tests. The pilots were between 17 and 28 years old. After the qualification tests, the pilots underwent extensive theoretical training and were then transferred to another base for practical training. By the end of the war, 1,375 personnel had been trained as *Kaiten* pilots.

Rear view showing the two propellers and the rudder. (© Pacific Fleet Submarine Museum)

Interior of the cramped and narrow *Kaiten 4* which was operated by one person. (© Pacific Fleet Submarine Museum)

Closeup of the conning tower, which was little more than a water deflector for the hatch to enter the interior. (NHHC)

The *Type 93* torpedo engine used for propulsion produced 550 hp. The maximum speed was 30 kn (34 mph/56 kph), the maximum range 42 nm (48 mi/78 km) at 12 kn (14 mph/22 kph). (NHHC)

Transport ships were to carry the *Kaiten* into its area of operation due to its limited range. (Former Imperial Japanese Navy)

Transport of several *Kaiten* torpedoes by submarines. Due to American naval and air supremacy from 1943/44 on, transportation on surface ships was often too risky. (Former Imperial Japanese Navy)

With 3,417 lb (1,550 kg) of explosives in the front section, the *Kaiten 1* design based on the prototype testing had a significantly higher destructive force than the original unmanned torpedo. Behind the explosive charge was the control station with the ballast, trim, and compensation tanks (cells). The latter compensated for the weight loss due to the fuel consumption caused by flooding with seawater. The centrally positioned control station had two access hatches: the first one was located on the top so that the pilot could enter normally from above. The second hatch was in the bottom so that the *Kaiten* could be transported into the operational area by large fleet submarines while submerged, thus enabling the pilot to transfer from the mother boat to the *Kaiten* for his mission.

Although the bottom hatch was also intended for the driver to exit through shortly before the collision with the target, getting out through this opening was only possible at very slow speed. As the *Kaiten* would then also have been rudderless, in case of enemy attacks or in case the target started moving, it was primarily used as a self-sacrificial weapon like kamikaze aircraft. Besides steering himself, the pilot could also set a course using the gyro instrument. Although the maximum diving depth was supposed to be 330 ft (100 m), leaks occurred during testing, so that from then on 200 ft (60 m) was specified as the maximum diving depth. About 100 units of this first variant were assembled at various shipyards from June 1944 on. In 1945, a slightly modified version with some 230 units was built.

Kaiten 2

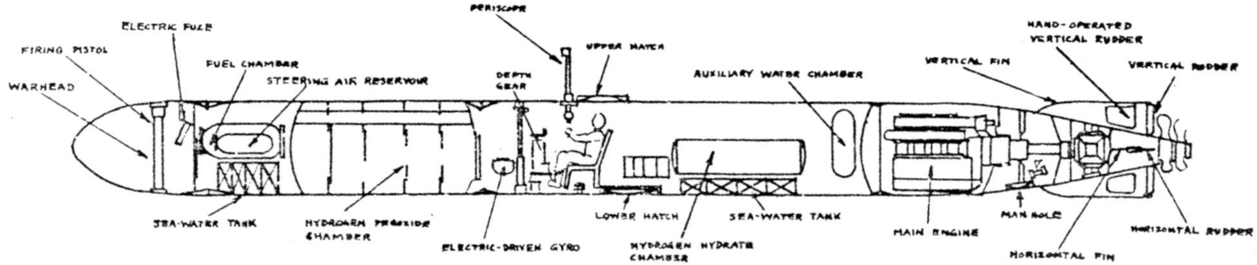

The *Kaiten 2* was to be equipped with a Walter propulsion system based on the German model and be capable of speeds of up to 40 kn (46 mph/74 kph). Due to technical problems, this variant did not go into series production. (NHHC)

Parallel to the start of series production, the prototype of the *Kaiten 2* was designed featuring slightly modified dimensions. In 1944, Germany had provided its ally Japan with technical documentation on the use of hydrogen peroxide for the Walter HWK 109–509 rocket engine, which was used in the Messerschmitt Me 163 interceptor aircraft. Since Mitsubishi had begun developing its own interceptor aircraft with hydrogen peroxide propulsion, the *Kaiten 2* was also to be equipped with such an engine. With a maximum output of 1,600 hp and a range of 45 nm (52 mi/83 km), the manned torpedo was to reach an underwater speed of up to 40 kn (46 mph/74 kph) and thus be at least as fast as most destroyers of the time, the nemeses of all submarines. Prototype testing showed that the propulsion system suffered from various weaknesses despite its promising high speed. In addition, it was difficult to build in series due to its complexity under the increasingly unfavorable war conditions. Moreover, a reliable supply of hydrogen peroxide was problematic. The overall situation led to the discontinuation of the project. The fate of the one or two prototypes is not known.

Kaiten 3

Depending on the source, a modified *Kaiten 3* prototype with an output of 1,800 hp and a top speed of 33 kn (38 mph/61 kph) is said to have been designed, but it did not go into series production either. Some sources report that this vehicle remained merely a planning study.

Kaiten 4

The *Kaiten 4* was equipped with a modified propulsion system that was to run on a mixture of oxygen and kerosene instead of hydrogen peroxide (like the original *Type 93* torpedo propulsion system). Due to the high oxygen consumption, the *Kaiten 4* only had a relatively short range of 21 nm (24 mi/39 km) but could dive to depths of up to 330 ft (100 m). The information on its maximum speed varies between 25 kn (29 mph/46 kph) and 37 kn (43 mph/69 kph). A slightly revised version was given the name *Kaiten 5*. Many experts considered *Kaiten 1*, which had meanwhile gone into series production and had entered service, to be the most balanced variant and all new developments required too many resources, production of the *Kaiten 4* and *Kaiten 5* was canceled after only some 50 units had been built.

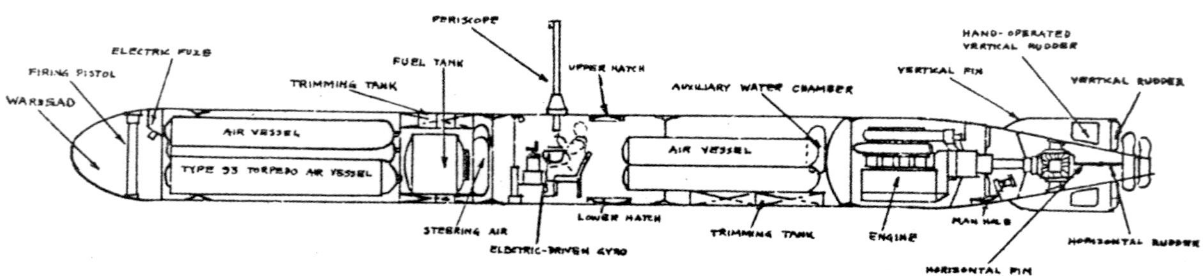

Like *Kaiten 2*, the *Kaiten 4* failed due to its overly complex and flawed propulsion system. (NHHC)

Kaiten 10

Due to the growing fear of an invasion of Japan by the Allies from early 1945, *Kaiten* production was to be increased to defend the islands. With the prevailing lack of resources, existing torpedoes therefore had to be converted by splitting them in the middle and inserting an additional control section for the pilot. The *Kaiten 10* designed this way was the only torpedo in the *Kaiten* fleet to have an electric propulsion. Although it was easy to construct, only about six were built by the end of the war. With a displacement of 3 tons, the weapon was 30 ft (9 m) long, had a diameter of 27.5 in (70 cm), carried a 660 lb (300 kg) warhead, and could dive about 66 ft (20 m) deep. Two lead-acid batteries supplied the electric motor with power and enabled a top speed of 7 kn (8 mph/13 kph) and a range of 1.9 nm (2.12 mi/3.5 km). Due to various technical problems, the *Kaiten 10* did not enter series production. The fate of the vehicles is unknown.

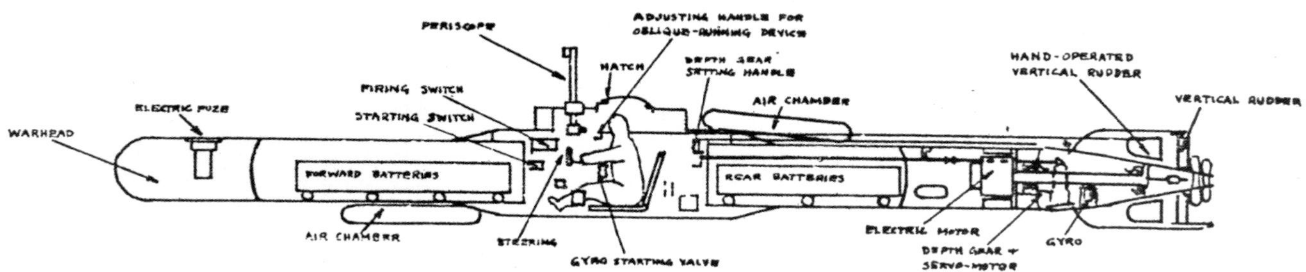

The easy-to-build *Kaiten 10* was considered an important means of defending the Japanese home islands in the event of an Allied invasion. However, it suffered from various technical problems. (NHHC)

Deployments

In November 1944, three Japanese mother submarines were to transport four *Kaiten 1* manned torpedoes to Ulithi Atoll to attack American ships anchored there. One of the submarines was sunk en route and another was only able to launch one *Kaiten* due to technical problems, but it missed its target. Although the four *Kaitens* of the third submarine began their attacks, only one of them was able to find a target and to sink the tanker USS *Mississinewa*, while the other three *Kaitens* were lost.

In July, around 120 *Kaitens* were positioned along the coast together with various submarines to attack the American invasion fleet. But after the two atomic bombs were dropped on Japan in early August 1945, the country surrendered, and no invasion took place. Although the Japanese had high expectations of the *Kaitens*, they were only able to sink a few ships with crippling losses of their own. A total of around 106 pilots lost their lives during their missions. Of the approximately 420 completed manned torpedoes, some have been preserved in museums in Japan and the United States.

The American tanker USS *Mississinewa* (burning in the background) was one of the few victims of the *Kaitens*. (NHHC)

After oil leaked from the wreck of the USS *Mississinewa* into Ulithi Lagoon, the U.S. Navy pumped out the remaining oil in 2003 to prevent a potential oil disaster. (NHHC)

The Most Successful *Kaiten* Attack

On July 24, 1945, the destroyer escort USS *Underhill* (DE-682) detected a Japanese reconnaissance aircraft circling an Allied convoy about 250 miles northeast of Cape Engaño off the island of Luzon in the Philippines. Remaining out of gun range, the Japanese pilot relayed the convoy's course to submarines operating in the area. One of these, *I-53*, carrying six *Kaitens*, released a dummy naval mine in the path of the convoy. When USS *Underhill*'s lookouts sighted the mine, the ship's commander ordered a general course change. When the destroyer escort tried to destroy the mine with its 20 mm guns and 30-caliber rifles, its crew realized the mine was a diversionary tactic by the Japanese submarines.

USS *Underhill* then noticed several sonar contacts, which were later revealed to be a Japanese submarine and several *Kaitens*. A depth-charge run was made which did not sink the submarine although it is suspected that it destroyed one of the *Kaitens*. Shortly after USS *Underhill* rammed one of the vessels (later revealed to be a *Kaiten*), while the ship was struck by a second *Kaiten* waiting in ambush. Both pilots were able to detonate their charges, one of which led to the explosion of the destroyer escort's boilers; the ship was torn in half by the subsequent explosions. The sinking resulted in the loss of almost half of USS *Underhill*'s crew, some 112 sailors.

Year/s of construction	1944–45
Builder/qty completed	Naval shipyards Hikari, Kure, Maizuru, Sasebo, Yokusuka/ca. 330 (all variants: 420)
Length	48.39 ft (14.75 m)
Beam	3.28 ft (1.0 m)
Draft	Unknown
Electric motor	550 hp
Propeller	2
Speed	30 kn
Displacement	8.3 tons
Range	42 nm at 12 kn
Crew	1
Diving depth	ca. 60–80 m
Armament	Explosives

3
Italy

The 1922 Washington Naval Treaty, which was signed following World War I to avoid another international naval arms race, had not only disadvantaged Japan, but also Italy. This international agreement had set the strength ratio between the United States, the United Kingdom, Japan, France, and Italy at 5:5:3:1.75:1.75.

Although Italy had thus achieved parity with its rival France, it would have been hopelessly outnumbered by a combined Anglo-French force. For this reason, the Italian navy and air force—like the Japanese and German military—attached great importance to the development of various small combat assets to compensate for treaty disadvantages (in the case of Germany, this was the Treaty of Versailles after its defeat in World War I).

Italy could already draw on a wealth of experience in the construction of such weapon systems, as it had already successfully deployed midget submarines, manned torpedoes, high-speed torpedo boats, and other vehicles during World War I. The combat value of manned torpedoes was demonstrated when an Italian *Mignatta* (leech) sank the Austrian battleship SMS *Viribus Unitis* with two explosive charges in the port of Pola, Istria, in November 1918.

From the mid-1930s onward, when Italy, then ruled by dictator Benito Mussolini, was already beginning to implement its expansionist plans in the Mediterranean and

Sinking of the Austrian battleship SMS *Viribus Unitis* by a mine in 1918, which had been placed under its hull by the crew of an Italian manned torpedo of the *Mignatta* type. (NHHC)

North Africa, the development of small warships was stepped up, as the Italian leadership was aware that there would be a confrontation with France and the United Kingdom in the near future, who would not tolerate Italy's expansion in the long term.

Midget Submarines

Type CA

From 1937 onward, Italy began the ambitious expansion of its small combat equipment, the effectiveness of which had already been demonstrated in the Mediterranean during World War I. The Caproni Works in Milan therefore designed a new midget submarine based on the previous *Type A* and *Type B* models built in 1915. This was to be used primarily for the defense of coastal areas and harbors. The two prototypes *CA-1* and *CA-2* (*Costiero A: Coastal Type A*), both completed in 1938, each had a length of 33 ft (10 m) and two 18 in (45 cm) torpedoes, which were mounted on both sides of the hull in recesses provided for this purpose. The propulsion consisted of a 60 hp MAN diesel engine for surface travel and a 25 hp E-engine when operating submerged.

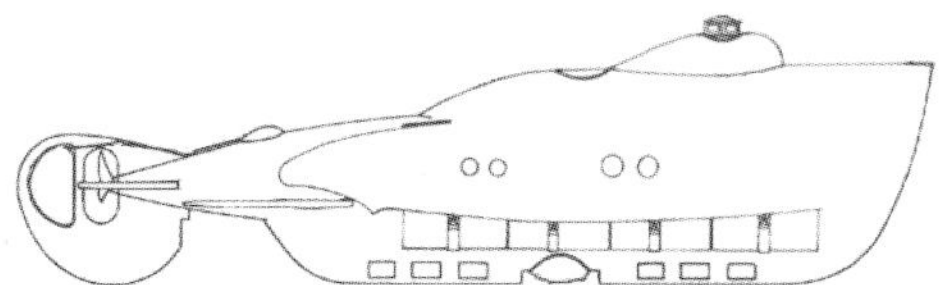

Simple drawing of the *Type CA* after its conversion in 1941/42. The most obvious external change is the modified and larger conning tower, which now had a plexiglass canopy.

The Italian *Type CA* submarines were designed by the Caproni Company and assembled in great secrecy. They were originally intended for coastal defense, but were later converted into secret attack boats, like the British *X-Craft*.

During sea trials, the technical equipment functioned well, but the seaworthiness proved to be poor. After both units were temporarily decommissioned, they were converted to carry combat swimmers (frogmen) and explosive charges. The previous diesel-electric drive gave way to a 28 hp Marelli electric motor used for surface and underwater travel. The range above water was now 70 nm (80 mi/130 km) at a cruising speed of only 2 kn (2.3 mph/3.7 kph), the maximum speed 7 kn (8 mph/13 kph). The speed for underwater travel is not known. Both boats were fitted with a lock for the entry and exit of frogmen and eight small explosive charges instead of torpedoes. The crew size increased from two to three. A plexiglass canopy replaced the previous periscope. Although the sea trials in 1942 made further modifications necessary, two more boats (*CA-3* and *CA-4*) were built. These were almost identical in construction but could dive slightly deeper to 230 ft (70 m).

Deployments

Three units of the *Type CA* only served as training boats and did not see any combat. With the Armistice of Cassibile (Sicily) between Italy and the United States/United Kingdom in September 1943, Italy broke from the alliance with Germany (after the Italians had overthrown dictator Benito Mussolini). This led to the scuttling of all four boats in La Spezia by their crews. Shortly afterward, however, they were raised and put back into service by the short-lived so-called Italian Social Republic proclaimed by Mussolini in northern Italy, a puppet state under German control. Later, experts from the Kriegsmarine dismantled the boats to study them for their own midget submarine designs.

CA-2, on the other hand, was to be transported to the waters of New York on the large submarine *Leonardo da Vinci* to attack ships or shipyards in the Hudson River. However, the mission never took place. *CA-2*, which was transferred to Bordeaux in France for this operation, was then placed under German command, but never saw action and was ultimately destroyed when the Germans eventually retreated.

A *Type CA* boat on a rail wagon. The low weight of around 13 tons and the length of around 33 ft (10 m) made transport by rail and truck possible. (BfZ)

Midget submarine *CA-1* or *CA-2* in 1938. The boats could reach 6.25 kn (7.2 mph/11.6 kph) above water and 5 kn (5.7 mph/9.3 kph) submerged. The radius of action was only 70 nm (80 mi/130 km) at 4 kn (4.6 mph/7.4 kph) above water and 57 nm (66 mi/105 km) (46 mph/74 km) at 3 kn (3.5 mph/5.6 kph) underwater. The diving depth was up to 180 ft (55 m). It was later rebuilt with a new propulsion system. (NHHC)

Planned Special Forces Attack on New York

Having invented the modern concept of using special forces to attack surface ships with *Mignatta* manned torpedoes in 1918, Italy led the world in terms of undersea special warfare into World War II. The Fascist nation entered the conflict on the Axis side and launched several naval special forces missions against British-controlled harbors in the Mediterranean as they lay within easy reach of Italy. However, one of the most ambitious midget submarine operations during the war would have been the Italian attack on the United States planned in 1943.

The idea was to transport a *Type CA* midget submarine to New York harbor piggybacked on the mother submarine *Leonardo da Vinci*. The *Type CA* then was to deliver "Gamma" frogmen to attack Allied shipping with limpet mines. This daring mission required the perfection of entirely new ways of operating special forces from submarines. As the U.S. mainland was generally thought to be out of range, an attack on New York would have had a strong psychological impact. The mission was only thwarted by timing and circumstances when the mother submarine *Leonardo da Vinci* was sunk by depth charges in May 1943 before the mission could be launched.

Year/s of construction	1938
Builder/qty completed	Caproni, Milan/4
Length	32.81 ft (10 m)
Beam	6.43 ft (1.96 m)
Diesel engine	60 hp
Electric motor	25 hp
Propeller	1
Speed ↑	6.25 kn
Speed ↓	5.0 kn
Displacement	13.5 tons ↑/ 16.4 tons ↓
Range ↑	70 nm at 4kn
Range ↓	57 nm at 3 kn
Crew	2
Diving depth	180 ft (55 m)
Armament	2 torpedoes

Type CB

Based on the experience gained with the *Type CA,* the successor *Type CB* was also built by Caproni in 1941. In contrast to their predecessors, the two prototypes *CB-1* and *CB-2* proved to be very seaworthy during testing. Like the German *Seehund,* the *Type CB* featured practically all the systems of a large submarine, including diving, control, and trim cells. Overall, the design was considered very successful. With a displacement of up to 46 tons (submerged), the boat was three times the size of its predecessor. A 90 hp Bota-Fraschini diesel engine enabled a maximum speed of 7.5 kn (8.6 mph/13.9 kph) above water, while the 100 hp Brown & Boveri electric engine was capable of 7 kn (8 mph/13 kph) when submerged (or 5 kn, depending on the source). The surface radius

With 22 completed units, the *Type CB* (*Costiero B: Coastal Type B*) was the most frequently built small submarine type of the Italian Navy. (NHHC)

A *Type CB* in port. Its appearance resembled that of a fast-attack motorboat. (NHHC)

A *Type CB* on a pier after being lifted out of the water. A second is still moored. (NHHC)

was given as an impressive 1,400 nm (1,612 mi/2,600 km), while the figures for the range when submerged varied greatly. As an alternative to their two 18 in (45 cm) torpedoes, the boats could carry two mines. The primary purpose included coastal defense and anti-submarine warfare.

After the delivery of the first boats, the Italian Navy saw the *Type CB* as a promising weapon and therefore decided on series production of at least 72 units. However, as other small weapons such as manned torpedoes (also known as human torpedoes) took up important resources, the number of boats to be built was reduced to about 50. Due to dwindling resources as the war situation deteriorated considerably from 1942/43 onward, only 12 boats were completed by the time of the Armistice of Cassibile in September 1943. A little later, 10 more units were assembled.

The midget submarine *CB-20* (later renamed *Mališan*) in the Nikola Tesla Museum of Technology in Zagreb, Croatia. It has undergone extensive restoration in recent years. (© Zvonimir Ambruš/Nikola Tesla Museum of Technology, Zagreb)

Front view of the restored *CB-20*. The submarine is one of the museum's most significant artifacts on display. (© Zvonimir Ambruš/Nikola Tesla Museum)

The primary armament of *CB-20* consisted of two 18 in (45 cm) torpedoes above the waterline on both sides of the hull. Alternatively, two mines could be carried. A machine gun was used for self-defense. (© Zvonimir Ambruš/Nikola Tesla Museum)

The relatively large conning tower has a window in its front side. (© Zvonimir Ambruš/Nikola Tesla Museum)

Rear view showing the combined design of the lower diving plane, rudder and propeller. In total, there were three diving planes.
(© Zvonimir Ambruš / Nikola Tesla Museum)

Closeup view of the rudder and propeller. The maximum speed submerged was up to 7 kn (8 mph/13 kph) and 7.5 kn (8.6 mph/13.9 kph) on the surface. (© Zvonimir Ambruš/Nikola Tesla Museum)

The open hatch on top of the midget submarine's conning tower. (© Zvonimir Ambruš/Nikola Tesla Museum)

The retractable periscope in the restored control center of *CB-20*. (© Zvonimir Ambruš/Nikola Tesla Museum)

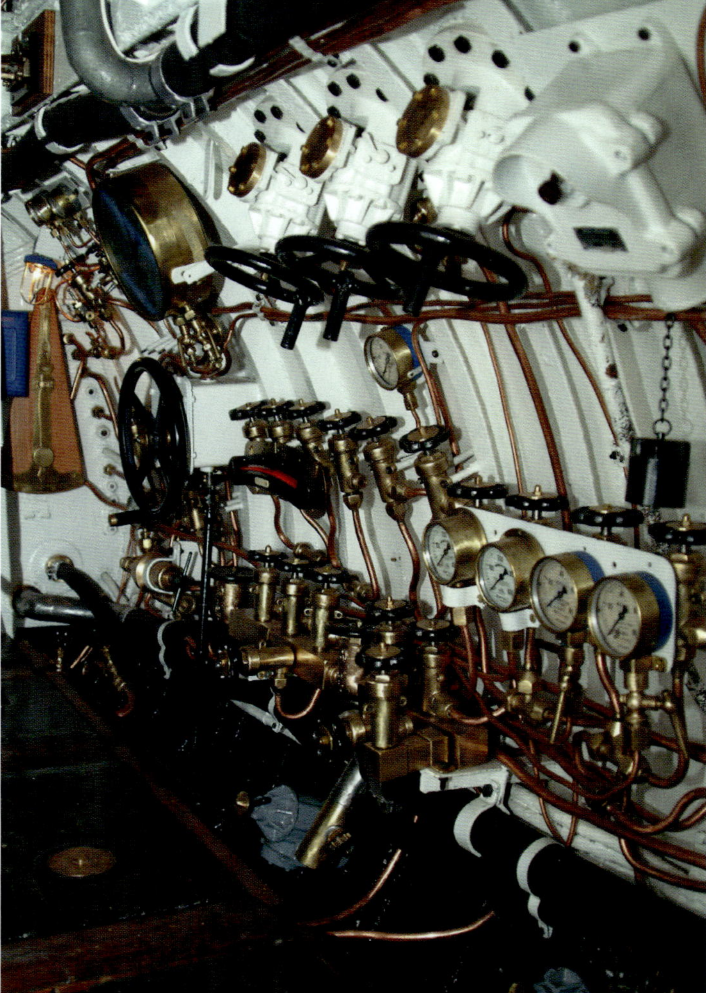

The beautifully restored control room with its various components to operate *CB-20*. (© Zvonimir Ambruš/Nikola Tesla Museum)

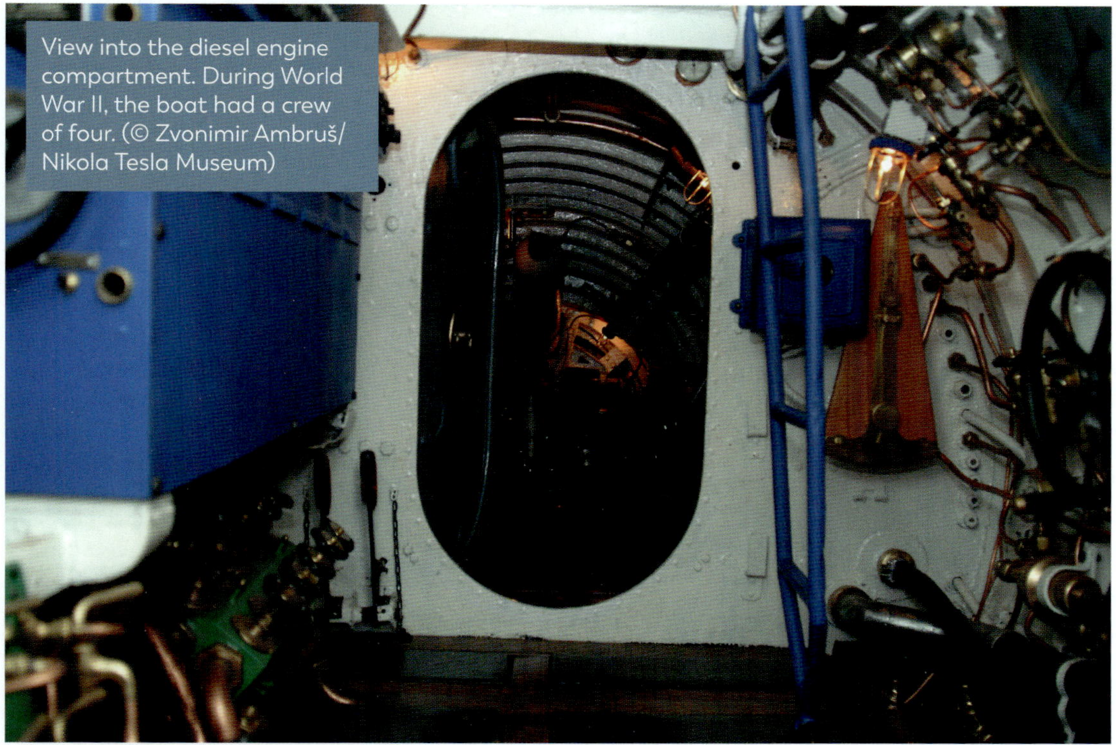

View into the diesel engine compartment. During World War II, the boat had a crew of four. (© Zvonimir Ambruš/Nikola Tesla Museum)

The diesel engine compartment of *CB-20*. While the Bota-Fraschini diesel engine had a power output of 90 hp, the Brown & Boveri electric engine could produce 100 hp. (© Zvonimir Ambruš/Nikola Tesla Museum)

Deployments

After the formation of the 1st Squadron with six boats (*CB-1* to *CB-6*) in the summer of 1941, this unit was to be used to protect the harbors of Naples and Salerno. Due to the lack of achievable missions, the boats were transferred to Constanta in Romania in the spring of 1942, from where they were deployed against the Soviet Black Sea Fleet. After the German conquest of the Crimean Peninsula, the ports of Sevastopol and Yalta served as additional bases. Depending on the source, *CB* boats succeeded in sinking one to three Soviet submarines of the *Shchuka*-class. During a Soviet attack on Yalta in June 1942, *CB-5* moored there was destroyed. On August 26, 1943, *CB-4* torpedoed and sank the Soviet submarine *Shch-203*.

The 2nd Squadron (*CB-7* to *CB-12*) was set up in Pola, Croatia (present-day Pula, Istria) in the summer of 1943. Five of the boats served on the Allied side for submarine-hunting exercises and training purposes after the armistice. *CB-7*, on the other hand, fell into the hands of the Germans, who first cannibalized and then destroyed it. The ten boats completed after the armistice (*CB-13* to *CB-22*) all served in the navy of Benito Mussolini's short-lived Italian Social Republic and, with two exceptions, fell victim to Allied air raids or ended up in scrapyards. *CB-20* was captured by Yugoslav partisans. After 1945, it served as the training boat *Mališan* (little boy) in the Yugoslav navy and was handed over to the Nikola Tesla Technical Museum in Zagreb, Croatia, in 1959. *CB-22* was raised and is now preserved in the Trieste Naval Museum.

Year/s of construction	1941–43
Builder/qty completed	Caproni, Milan/22
Length	49.21 ft (15.0 m)
Beam	98.43 ft (30 m)
Diesel engine	90 hp
Electric motor	100 hp
Propeller	1
Speed ↑	7.5 kn
Speed ↓	5–7 kn
Displacement	36 tons ↑/ 45 tons ↓
Range ↑	ca. 1,400 nm at 5 kn
Range ↓	Unknown
Crew	4
Diving depth	180 ft (55 m)
Armament	2 torpedoes or 2 mines; 1 machine gun

Type CC

In 1942, the Italian Navy demanded a small submarine with a displacement of 100 tons which could operate in extended coastal areas and be produced in large numbers. At the beginning of 1943, the Caproni Works in Milan therefore began work on the *Type CC* design. The Cantieri Riuniti dell'Adriatico (CRDA) shipyard in Monfalcone received the same order from the navy and named its concept *Type CM*. This meant that the navy immediately had an alternative to hand in the event of an unsuccessful design. Caproni began building three prototypes which had all the systems of a large submarine, including diving, control, and trim cells. The armament consisted of three 18 in (45 cm) bow torpedo tubes. The crew consisted of two officers and six men to allow for longer missions through uninterrupted duty rotation. With a maximum displacement of 117 tons and a length of 108 ft (33 m), the diving depth was to be up to 260 ft (80 m). The two 350 hp Fiat diesel engines were to enable a maximum speed of 16 kn (18.4 mph/30 kph) above water, with the two 60 hp CRDA electric engines achieving 9 kn (10.4 mph/16.7 kph) when submerged. The maximum range above water was to be 1,200 nm (1,380 mi/2,220 km) at 10 kn (11.5 mph/18.5 kph) and 70 nm (80 mi/130 km) at 4 kn (4.6 mph/7.4 kph) when submerged. A few days after the Armistice of Cassibile in September 1943, construction of the three boats (*CC-1* to *CC-3*) was halted and they were eventually demolished.

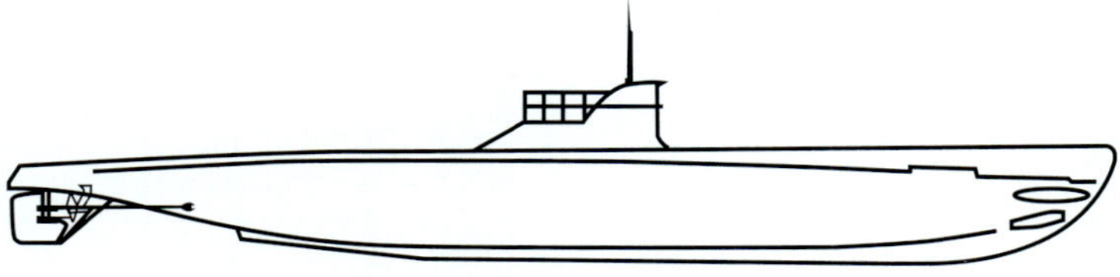

The design of the *Type CC* (*Costiero Caproni: Caproni Coastal Type*) envisaged a small boat armed with three torpedoes, larger than midget submarines.

Type CD

At the beginning of 1942, the Italian Navy commissioned the aircraft and naval engineer Secondo Campini to develop a single-seater midget submarine with water-jet propulsion for diving. Campini was experienced in this field, as he had already designed and successfully tested a boat with such an engine. The *Type CD* was to be built by the Caproni Works in Milan.

The design envisaged a torpedo-like craft with a shape designed entirely for underwater use. The fully retractable, 1-meter-high conning tower (for diving) was placed on the stern section. The armament consisted of two 18 in (45 cm) torpedoes mounted under the hull. A conventional 60 hp Carraro diesel engine was used for surface travel, enabling a top speed of 11.5 kn (13.2 mph/21.3 kph; range unknown). The water-jet propulsion for underwater travel, on the other hand, was innovative. The 600 hp turbine powered by an oxygen-gas mixture sucked in water under the hull and expelled it through nozzles at the stern, so that the generated recoil propelled the boat. In addition to a planned maximum speed of 30 kn (34.5 mph/55.6 kph), this propulsion system also had the advantage that the small craft was difficult to detect by acoustic detection systems due to the lack of propeller noise. In addition to a version equipped with torpedoes, a minelayer and a special boat with gripper arms for cutting through net barriers were also to be built.

Due to a shortage of materials and parallel projects at Caprioni, the *Type CD* did not progress beyond the experimental stage. The fate of the prototypes tested in Lake Garda is unclear. Depending on the source, one or even both boats are said to have been sunk there by the Germans in 1945. According to other sources, American troops were able to recover a prototype and transferred it to the United States for further examination.

Year/s of construction	1942–43
Builder / qty completed	Caproni, Milan / 2
Length	36.09 ft (11 m)
Beam	2.95 ft (0.9 m)
Diesel engine	60 hp
Electric motor	600 hp
Propeller	-
Speed ↑	11.5 kn
Speed ↓	Up to 30 kn
Displacement	5.6 tons ↑/ 5.83 tons ↓
Range ↑	Unknown
Range ↓	Unknown
Crew	1
Diving depth	Unknown
Armament	2 torpedoes or mines

The large submarine *Liuzzi*. The midget submarines of the types *CC*, *CD*, and *CM* featured most of the technical equipment used on larger boats. (NHHC)

Type CM

In addition to Caproni's *Type CC*, the *Type CM* was also built by CRDA (Cantieri Riuniti dell'Adriatico) shipyard in Monfalcone in early 1943 in response to the navy's demand for a 100-ton small submarine with a crew of eight. This design, armed with two 18 in (45 cm) bow torpedoes, was to have a maximum displacement of 114 tons (submerged) with a length of just under 108 ft (33 m). The propulsion consisted of two Fiat diesel engines with 330 hp each and two CRDA electric motors with 60 hp each. The boat was to reach 14 kn (16.1 mph/26 kph) above water and 6 kn to 9 kn (6.9 mph to 10.4 mph/11 kph to 17 kph) submerged. The maximum range for surface travel was to be up to 2,000 nm (2,602 mi/3,700 km) or less (depending on the source) at 10 kn (11.5 mph/18.5 kph) and 70 nm (80 mi/130 km) at 4 kn (4.6 mph/7.4 kph) underwater.

The maximum diving depth was to be 260 ft (80 m). Two machine guns were to be used for self-defense during surface operations. The three boats under construction were given the designations *CM-1*, *CM-2* and *CM-3*. The abbreviation "CM" stood for *Costiero Monfalcone* (*Monfalcone Coastal Type*). After the Armistice of Cassibile between Italy and the Allies in September 1943, the three boats, still under construction, were seized by the German Kriegsmarine, which handed them over to the Marina Nazionale Repubblicana of Benito Mussolini's short-lived Italian Social Republic (a German puppet state) in October. *CM-1* was eventually commissioned in January 1945, but did not see any action and was eventually scrapped after the war. *CM-2* was never completed and severely damaged during an Allied air raid in May 1944. When the wreck was seized by the Germans in April 1945, they scuttled it. After raising *CM-2* in 1950, most of it was broken up, while several parts ended up in the Trieste Military Museum. After the Armistice of Cassibile, *CM-3* was still under construction, but once in German hands, it was stripped down and its parts were used to complete the sister boats *CM-1* and *CM-2*. The remaining sections were scrapped after the war.

CM-1 ready for its launch. It never saw any combat action. (Former Regia Marina)

CM-1 after World War II. The shape resembled that of the larger German *Type VII* boat. (Former Regia Marina)

Year/s of construction	1943
Builder/qty completed	CRDA, Monfalcone/3
Length	108.1 ft (32.95 m)
Beam	9.48 ft (2.89 m)
Draft	9.09 ft (2.77 m)
Diesel engine	2 × 330 hp
Electric motor	2 × 60 hp
Propeller	2
Speed ↑	14 kn
Speed ↓	6–9 kn
Displacement	92 tons ↑/114 tons ↓
Range ↑	Up to 2,000 nm at 10 nm
Range ↓	70 nm at 4 kn
Crew	8
Diving depth	262 ft (80 m)
Armament	2 torpedoes and 2 machine guns

In Profile:
Italian Midget Submarines and Manned Torpedoes

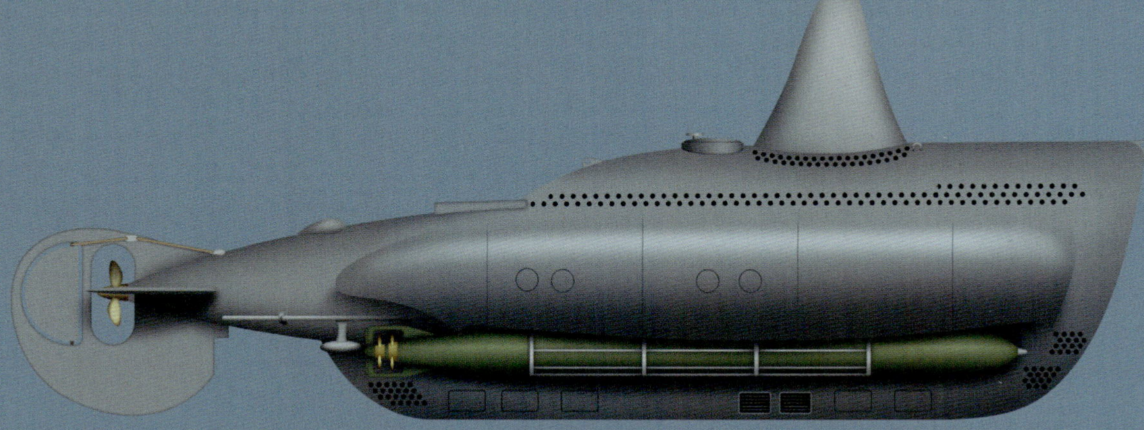

Type CA Midget Submarine

Designed by the Caproni Company, the *CAs* were originally intended for coastal defense but were later converted into secret attack boats. The low weight of 13 tons and the length of around 33 ft (10 m) made transport by rail and truck possible. The boats could reach 6.25 kn (7.2 mph/11.6 kph) above water and 5 kn (5.7 mph/9.3 kph) submerged. The radius of action was only 70 nm (80 mi/130 km) at 4 kn (4.6 mph/7.4 kph) above water and 57 nm (66 mi/105 km) (46 mph/74 kph) at 3 kn (3.5 mph/5.6 kph) underwater. The diving depth was up to 180 ft (55 m). A daring special forces-type raid was planned with a *CA-2*, to be transported by the large submarine *Leonardo da Vinci* to attack ships or shipyards in the Hudson River. The plan came to nought when the *Leonardo da Vinci* was sunk before the raid could take place.

Type SLC (Maiale)

Italy led the way with manned torpedoes, having successfully sunk the Austrian battleship SMS *Viribus Unitis*, among others, during World War I. In the 1930s, the *SLC* (*siluro a lenta corsa* or slow-running torpedo) was developed. Due to its sluggishness in the water, it was nicknamed *Maiale* (pig). Two operators called "torpedo riders" sat one behind the other on the 22 ft (6.7 m) long torpedo in seats and footrests. The one at the front was the commander and helmsman, while the one at the rear was responsible for placing the explosive charge at the target. At the front of the bow was the detachable 550 lb or 250 kg (later 660 lb or 300 kg) explosive charge and behind it a trim tank.

Manned Torpedoes

Type SLC (Maiale)

Italy had already developed manned torpedoes during World War I and successfully used them to sink the Austrian battleship SMS *Viribus Unitis*, among others. Based on this experience, a new vehicle was developed in the mid-1930s with the designation *SLC* (*siluro a lenta corsa* or slow-running torpedo). After the completion of two prototypes at the San Bartolomeo Underwater Weapons Factory in La Spezia in 1935, both were tested. As the results were satisfactory, series production began after some delay and a training center was set up for the future "torpedo riders."

The *Type SLC (Maiale)* was based on the *Mignatta* used in World War I, but it had the advantage of being capable of diving. (U.S. Navy)

Stern view of the *SLC*. The small hull was a torpedo. (U.S. Navy)

The two men sat one behind the other on the 22 ft (6.7 m) long torpedo in seats and footrests. The one at the front was the commander and helmsman, while the one at the rear was responsible for placing the explosive charge at the target. At the front of the bow was the detachable 550 lb or 250 kg (later 660 lb or 300 kg) explosive charge and behind it a trim tank. The battery and the 1.1 hp electric motor were in the center of the fuselage. The stern contained a counterbalance tank (which was intended to balance the *SLC*

The crew wore a light diving suit. Breathing was made possible by an oxygen diving device with a mouthpiece attached to the body. (U.S. Navy)

While the commander/helmsman (right) sat at the front, the operations man, who had to place the explosive charge at the target, sat at the rear. (U.S. Navy)

The *SLC* could dive within seven seconds. The front seat ("cockpit") had a protective cover (fairing) as a breakwater. The controls were located underneath. (U.S. Navy)

The "cockpit" with the steering wheel, depth gauge, compass, voltmeter, ammeter, and pressure gauge. These displays had illuminated numbers for better legibility. (U.S. Navy)

after the explosive charge had been removed), the shaft tunnel, the drive propeller, and the torpedo-type rudder and diving plane. The crew's oxygen breathing apparatus had a six-hour supply and only worked up to a depth of 50 ft (15 m). However, the use of these devices was dangerous, as accidents frequently occurred due to carbon dioxide poisoning and breathing problems caused by excessive water pressure. This happened when the torpedo riders exceeded the maximum depth of 50 ft during their missions and the breathing "bag" was crushed by the higher water pressure. This could lead to death by asphyxiation. For this reason, compressed-air diving equipment was introduced, which worked safely down to a depth of 130 ft (40 m), as it provided compressed air for inhalation regardless of the water pressure. The exhaled carbon dioxide escaped into the water through filters built into the mouthpiece.

Riding on a Torpedo

During World War II, manned torpedoes (also known as human torpedoes) were a type of diver propulsion vehicle on which the diver rode, generally in a seated position behind a fairing. The basic concept is still in use. More broadly, the term "manned torpedo" referred to vehicles which are today considered "wet submarines or diver propulsion vehicles" for either military or recreational divers. Midget submarines supporting frogman operations (with or without airlocks), if used to transport equipment and frogmen clinging to their exterior or as underwater tugs, also blur the line between "manned torpedoes" and more sophisticated and complex underwater vehicles.

Due to its short range of only 10 nm (11.5 mi/18.5 km) and low speed of 2.5 kn (2.9 mph/4.6 kph), the *SLC* had to be used primarily at night. In addition, it had to be transported to the area of deployment (usually a port or bay) by transport or towing vessels or on the deck of mother submarines in specially developed pressure

The *SLC* (right) approaches the anchored enemy ship and positions itself under the hull. (U.S. Navy)

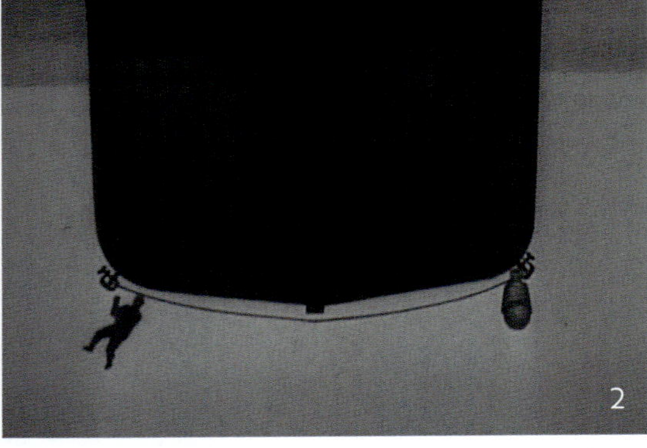

The man gets out and attaches a wire rope from one side of the ship's bottom to the other using magnets. (U.S. Navy)

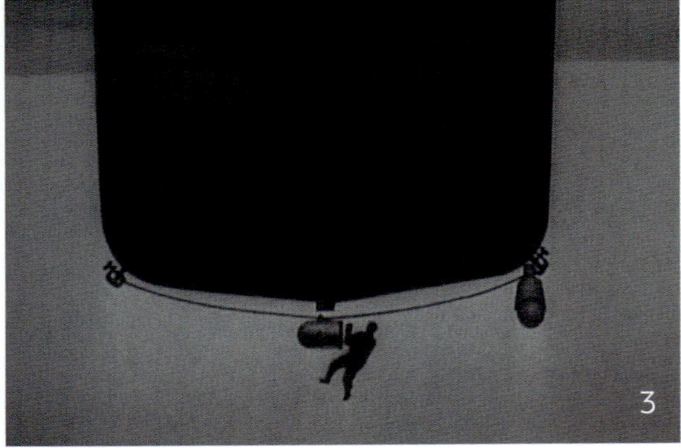

He then detaches the 550 lb (250 kg) explosive from the bow of the *SLC* and moves it directly under the ship's keel while hanging on the rope. After the timer fuze is set, he returns to the *SLC*, which escapes to safety. The explosion breaks the keel or tears a hole in the hull and sinks the target. (U.S. Navy)

vessels. The use of these containers was necessary because enemy aircraft could detect submerged boats to a depth of about 160 ft (50 m) in the Mediterranean. The use of these containers therefore enabled the mother submarines to dive deeper with the *SLC* vehicles without them being destroyed by the water pressure. In the area of deployment, the submarines then surfaced or remained at periscope depth so that the *SLC* crews could board their vehicles.

The *SLC* then approached its target as slowly as possible to avoid a treacherous wake. About 160 ft (50 m) in front of the enemy ship, it then dived completely to take up its position directly under the hull of the target. One of the torpedo riders then detached the explosive charge from the *SLC*'s bow and attached it to the target using magnets (see sequence of pictures). The time fuze could be set to a delay time of 150 minutes. After placing the explosive charge, the *SLC* crew would try to escape to rendezvous with a ship or submarine. Alternatively, they would sink their vehicle themselves, surrender, and hope to be captured alive.

Some Operations

Between Italy's entry into World War II in 1940 and the Armistice of Cassibile in September 1943, numerous *SLC* operations were carried out against Allied ships and other targets. Some of these operations took place in coordination with speedboats, explosive boats, or frogmen.

On September 21, 1941, the mother submarine *Scirè* transported three *SLC* manned torpedoes to the coast of Gibraltar, where they succeeded in sinking the two tankers *Fiona Shell* and *Denbydale* as well as the cargo

After being attacked by Italian *SLC* manned torpedoes, the British battleships HMS *Queen Elizabeth* (shown here) and HMS *Valiant* both sank to the shallow bottom in the harbor of Alexandria, Egypt. If the attack had taken place in a deeper bay or on the open sea, both battleships would most likely have been lost. (NHHC)

ship *Durham*. On December 18, 1941, *Scirè* launched three *SLC*s off the Egyptian port of Alexandria. There they attacked the two British battleships HMS *Queen Elizabeth* and HMS *Valiant*, both of which sank to the bottom in shallow water after the charges exploded. It took several months before the two ships were operational again. In addition, the Norwegian tanker *Sagona* and the destroyer *Jervis* were damaged. This spectacular success in just one day marked the peak of the *SLC* operations.

After the Armistice of Cassibile, some of the vehicles ended up in the hands of the navy of Mussolini's short-lived Italian Social Republic and thus under German control. Although they were handed over to the Kriegsmarine small combat units, no operations are known (so far). In 1942, the British Royal Navy was able to salvage and study some of those that had sunk near Gibraltar as well as one that had been washed ashore. These served in part as a model for the British manned torpedo *Chariot*. The *SLC* manned torpedoes proved to be successful as they destroyed three warships, about 12 merchant ships (a total of 60,000 tons, depending on the source), and damaged numerous other vessels. The number of units built is estimated at 43 to 51. The loss rate of the crews is not known. Today, several *SLC* manned torpedoes are preserved in various museums.

Year/s of construction	1940–43 (prototype 1935)
Builder/qty completed	San Bartolomeo Underwater Weapons Factory, La Spezia/43–51
Length	21.98 ft (6.7 m)
Beam	1.74 ft (0.53 m)
Electric motor	1.1 hp
Propeller	1
Speed	2.5 kn
Displacement	Unknown
Range	10 nm
Crew	2
Diving depth	100–130 ft (30–40 m)
Armament	551–661 lb (250–300 kg) of explosives

Type SBB

In 1943, based on practical experience with the successful *SLC*, a modified version was built with the designation *SBB* (*Siluro San Bartolomeo* or *Torpedo Type San Bartolomeo*). The two torpedo riders now sat on a slightly larger vehicle, which was more streamlined and, at 4.5 kn (5.2 mph/8.3 kph), faster underwater than its predecessor. Depending on the source, the maximum range was up to 70 nm (80 mi/130 km). The armament initially consisted of a detachable 660 lb (300 kg) explosive charge in the bow. Later versions were to be able to

Compared to its predecessor, the *SBB* had an optimized shape for diving operations. (U.S. Navy)

The propeller at the stern had a ring-shaped protection against damage. (U.S. Navy)

View into the cockpit at the front of the *SBB*. (U.S. Navy)

If the *SBB* crew were discovered during a mission, they were completely exposed to enemy fire. (U.S. Navy)

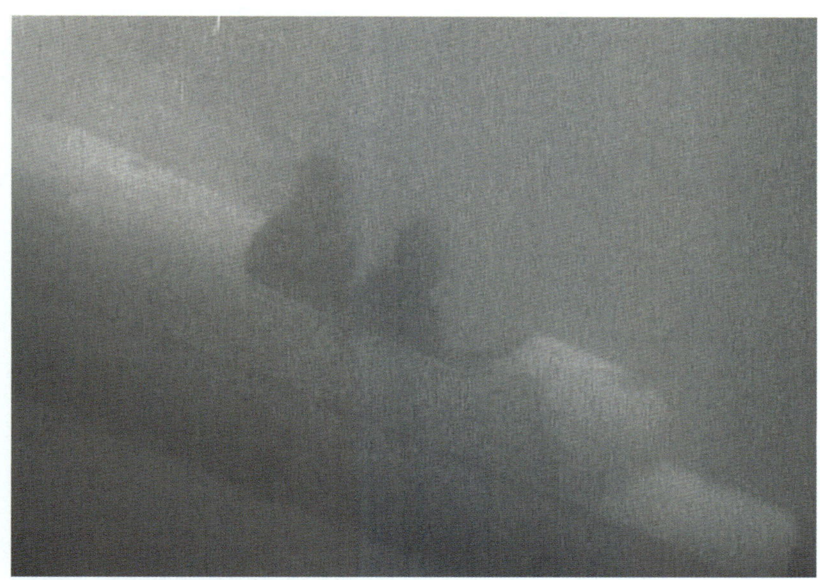

The *SBB* could dive to a depth of 100 ft (30 m). (U.S. Navy)

carry a single 880 lb (400 kg) version or two 440 lb (200 kg) warheads. By the time of the armistice, only nine vehicles had been completed (or fewer, depending on the source). Some were to be deployed from La Spezia in an attack on British-controlled Gibraltar, but the end of hostilities prevented this plan. A preserved *SBB* is on display at the British Royal Navy Submarine Museum in Gosport.

Year/s of construction	1943
Builder/qty completed	San Bartolomeo Underwater Weapons Factory, La Spezia/ca. 9
Length	22.21 ft (6.77 m)
Beam	2.59 ft (ca. 0.79 m)
Electric motor	7.5 hp
Propeller	1
Speed ↑	2.3 kn
Speed ↓	4.5 kn
Displacement	Unknown
Range	Up to 70 nm
Crew	2
Diving depth	ca. 100 ft (30 m)
Armament	661–882 lb (300–400 kg) of explosives

4
United Kingdom

During World War I, the British officer Max Horton had the idea of developing midget submarines to attack the German High Seas Fleet in North Sea ports. Instead, the Royal Navy decided to build speedboats armed with torpedoes and only had a few experimental submarines built. In the 1920s, Horton proposed the concept of a new midget submarine type, which was to be deployed by mother ships, but this was also (initially) not well received. In the following decade, submarine commander C. Varley presented the idea of a manned (human) torpedo, but this was rejected as too "suicidal." His design for a two-man midget submarine in 1939 also failed to make it past the drawing board. From 1940, however, the attitude of the British Admiralty changed. Norway, which had been occupied by the Germans, with its fjords, and France, which was also occupied, with its nearby coasts, offered promising opportunities for use against German ships in harbors and supply lines. The midget submarines and manned torpedoes now to be developed were to be used mostly in coastal waters and bays.

The Irish submarine pioneer John P. Holland. From 1900, he designed midget submarines for the U.S. Navy, and later for the Royal Navy. Some of these formed the basis for the British *X-Craft*, which saw service in World War II. (NHHC)

Midget Submarines

X-Craft

Even before the outbreak of World War II in Europe in 1939, the development of the *X-Craft* type began as a midget submarine for special operations in coastal waters. The two prototypes were given the designations *X-3* and *X-4*, as the numbers *X-1* (a submarine cruiser) and *X-2* (a captured German submarine of the *Type VIIC*) had already been assigned. After their completion and testing, final assembly began at Vickers-Armstrongs in December 1942, as some of the components came from various suppliers. In addition to the two prototypes, a further 18 units were built, six of which were used as training boats.

As the *X-Craft* had no conning tower, it was very difficult for the enemy to spot it on the surface, but could easily fill up with water if the hatch was kept open in rough seas. (Royal Navy/Ministry of Defence)

Depiction of an *X-Craft* operating at periscope depth. (© Faller)

A crewmember (probably the commander) at the periscope. The crew consisted of four men. As there were no sanitary facilities on board, a container was used as a toilet. (Royal Navy/Ministry of Defence)

Almost 52 ft (16 m) long and displacing up to 30 tons, the *X-Craft* consisted of four compartments: in the bow was a small sleeping and storage room, behind this was the control center with all controls, followed by a narrow exit airlock through which a diver could leave the boat while submerged. The engine room with the diesel and electric drive was in the stern. The boat had an extendable periscope, a gyrocompass for navigation and a listening device for detecting ships and submarines. The well-designed *X-Craft* featured practically all the technical systems of large submarines, including diving, control, and trim cells.

A 42 hp four-cylinder Gardner diesel engine, which was also used in the London double-decker buses, was the propulsion system for surface travel. It enabled a top speed of 6.5 kn (7.5 mph/12 kph) and a cruising range of around 500 nm (575 mi/926 km). A 30 hp Keith-Blackman electric motor was used for underwater operations, which drew its energy from a 112-cell lead accumulator in the bow compartment. The maximum speed was 5.5 kn (6.3 mph/10 kph) and the maximum range at a cruising speed of 2.2 kn (2.5 mph/4 kph) was around 82 nm (94 mi/152 km). The armament consisted of two side-mounted jettisonable bottom mines, each with 4,480 lb (2,032 kg) of Amatex explosives. The mines were dropped by a crank inside the boat and activated by a time fuze.

During a mission, the four-man crew consisted of the commander (navigation and operation of the periscope), the first lieutenant (ship's command and control), the engineer (monitoring of the boat's technical systems and maintenance of the drive), and the combat diver. The latter exited through the pressure lock, to attach additional limpet mines to ships or other targets or to cut barrage nets.

The *X-Craft* in popular culture

The novel *Surface with Daring*, written by Douglas Reeman in 1976, features a fictionalized account of *X-class* (*X-Craft*) midget submarines and its brave crews, especially *XE-16* performing several highly secret operations in occupied Europe during World War II. A 2006 Alexander Fullerton novel, *The Gatecrashers*, features a fictionalized account of *X-class* midget submarines laying explosive charges to damage the German battleship *Tirpitz*.

Deployments

Due to their short range, *X-Craft* midget submarines usually had to travel to the deployment area in tow of large submarines. They only covered the last few nautical miles under their own power. While the *X-Craft* carried out their operations, the mother submarines waited near the deployment area at an agreed rendezvous point to be able to tow the returning *X-Craft* back to base.

While these vehicles saw action in various theaters, their attack on the German battleship *Tirpitz* is the best-known operation. As the powerful warship was to attack the Allied supply convoys from German-occupied Norway on their way from America or Scotland to Murmansk, Russia, it posed a permanent threat. After extensive preparations, three *X-Craft* (*X-5*, *X-6*, and *X-7*) were therefore to attack the *Tirpitz* at its new berth in the Kåfjord and neutralize it as part of Operation *Source*. While *X-5* was already lost during the approach, *X-6* and *X-7* each succeeded in laying two mines with time-fuze triggers underneath the battleship. Although the Germans discovered the two midget submarines and took their crews prisoner (after they had scuttled *X-6* and *X-7* themselves), the time remaining until the mines were detonated was too short to generate the necessary

In September 1943, two *X-Craft* managed to place their mines underneath the *Tirpitz* and, by detonating them, damaged the German battleship to such an extent that it was not operational for months. (NHHC)

steam pressure on the *Tirpitz* to leave the berth. Therefore, the ship could only be moved slightly to one side by hauling in the lines by operating the fore and aft capstans. The subsequent explosion damaged the hull and shifted the engines on their foundations, so that the *Tirpitz* was not operational until spring 1944. Although further submarine attacks were planned on the battleship, it later fell victim to an air raid. After salvaging the sunken *X-Craft* and its subsequent investigation by German engineers, the Kriegsmarine decided to develop similar submarines.

A Useful Tool

A hand-held, hydraulically-powered net-cutter was used by *X-Craft* divers to cut through torpedo nets protecting enemy harbors.

Operation *Overlord*

During the preparations for the Allied landings in Normandy in June 1944, an *X-Craft* was used to deploy divers off the French coast at night to take soil samples at various locations to determine the best landing points for floatable tanks and other vehicles. It had become apparent that the tracks of these vehicles did not work on all surfaces and therefore, in the worst case, "dug themselves in," making them an easy target for the German defenders and their artillery on the beach. During the landings on June 6, *X-20* and *X-23*, equipped with position lights, were used to mark the extreme left and right positions of the British and Canadian landing zones, thus acting as navigational beacons to help the invasion fleet land on the correct beaches (Operation *Gambit*). Both boats were also equipped with radio beacons and echo sounders to help direct British and Canadian ships to the suitable positions on *Sword* and *Juno* beaches. Oxygen bottles enabled the crews to remain submerged for 64 hours of the 76 total hours at sea.

While seven midget submarines were lost during various missions, the surviving boats were decommissioned and scrapped after the end of the war. The only fully preserved example is *X-24*, which is now on display at the British Royal Navy Submarine Museum in Gosport.

X-24 in the British Royal Navy Submarine Museum in Gosport. In April 1944, it sank the German supply ship *Bärenfels* in the Norwegian port of Bergen. (© Royal Navy Submarine Museum)

Soil Samples for a Preparatory D-Day Mission

In January 1944, less than five months before the Allied invasion of Normandy, *X-20* was ordered to take surveys of the potential landing beaches. Commanded by Lieutenant K. R. Hudspeth, the boat spent four days off the French coast performing periscope reconnaissance of the shoreline and echo-soundings during daytime. Each night, *X-20* approached the beach, and two divers swam ashore collecting soil samples in condoms to determine the best landing points.

Both men went ashore on two nights surveying the beaches at Vierville-sur-Mer, Moulins St. Laurent, and Colleville-sur-Mer, later codenamed *Omaha* Beach for the American landing forces. On the third night, the divers were due to go ashore off the Orne Estuary (later codenamed *Sword* Beach for the British landing forces), but at this point the crew and divers were too exhausted as they had been living on little more than Benzedrine tablets. In addition, the worsening weather conditions forced Lieutenant Hudspeth to return to base.

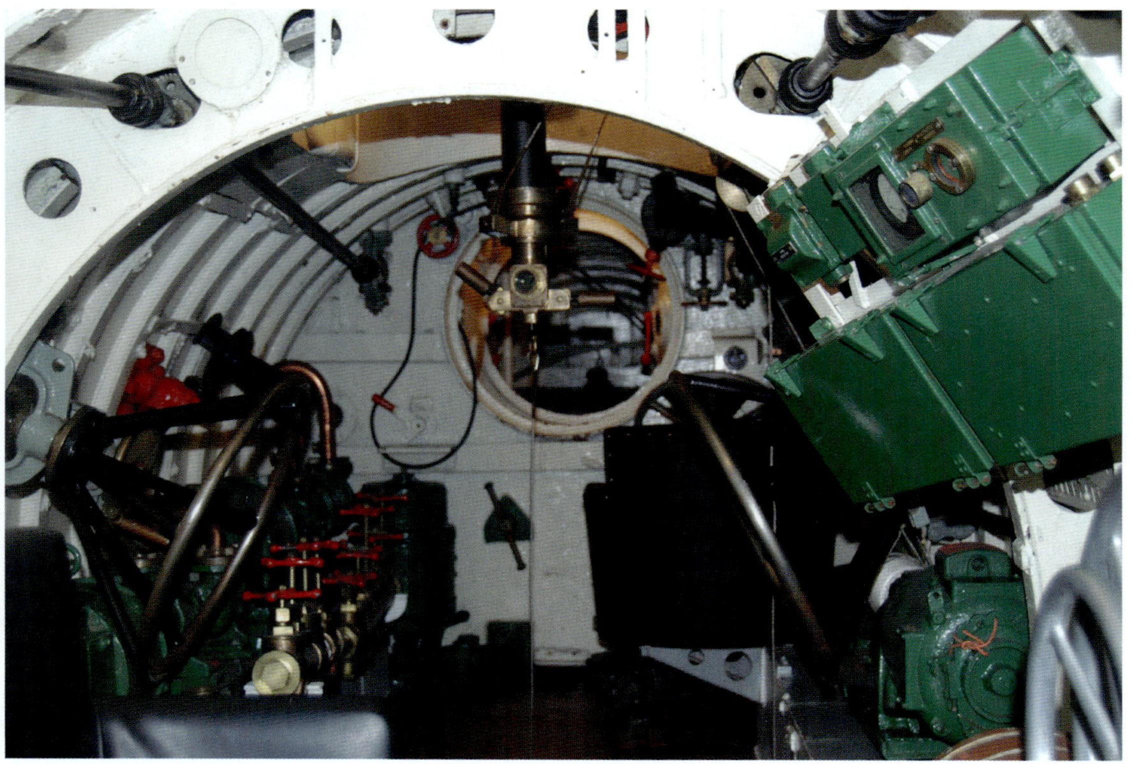

View of the interior of the lovingly restored *X-24*. Parts of other *X-Craft* boats are preserved in other museums. (© Royal Navy Submarine Museum)

After World War II all *X-Craft* were declared surplus and sent to the Royal Naval Construction Establishment in Rosyth. There they were to be employed in a series of tests to explore the effects on midget submarines. This included diving to collapse depth and being exposed to artillery fire as well as to non-contact charges. Once the testing was completed in 1947, the submarines (most likely *K-4* and *K-17*) that were used for the test-firing at Gullan Sand (east of Edinburgh) were left on the beach where they remain to this day. (© Iain Jack)

The two submarine wrecks have sunk into the sand with most of their outer hulls rusted away.
(© Iain Jack)

Year/s of construction	1942
Builder/qty completed	Vickers-Armstrongs/20
Length	51.25 ft (15.62 m)
Beam	5.74 ft (1.75 m)
Diesel engine	42 hp
Electric motor	30 hp
Propeller	1
Speed ↑	6.5 kn
Speed ↓	5.5 kn
Displacement	27 tons ↑/30 tons ↓
Range ↑	ca. 500 nm
Range ↓	82 nm at 2 kn
Crew	4
Diving depth	ca. 295 ft (90 m)
Armament	2 mines

XE-Craft

In 1944, a slightly modified successor designated the *XE-Craft* was built based on the successful *X-Craft*. In addition to its jettisonable bottom mines, it could also carry six 20 lb (9 kg) magnetic mines, which the combat diver was to attach to the target. From July 1945, the boats were used exclusively in the Far East during the final phase of the Pacific War. There, four of them operated together with their depot ship HMS *Bonaventure* and large submarines from Malaya (now Malaysia). On July 31, the submarine HMS *Spearhead* towed *XE-4* to the Mekong Delta at the southern tip of Vietnam as part of Operation *Sabre*. From there it travelled to the Saigon River, where its diver disembarked and cut the Japanese underwater communication cables between Saigon and Hong Kong. In August 1945, *XE-5* also succeeded in cutting the cable connection between Hong Kong and Singapore (Operation *Foil*).

XE-4 released one or two divers into the Saigon River in July 1945 to cut the Japanese underwater communication cables between Saigon and Hong Kong. (Australian War Memorial/114892)

XE-8 on display at the Chatham Historic Dockyard amid various other maritime artifacts. The upper parts of the outer hull are missing. (© Chatham Historic Dockyard Trust)

Bow view of *XE-8*, which was raised after 21 years on the ocean floor. (© Chatham Historic Dockyard Trust)

Although 12 units (*XE-1* to *XE-12*) were built in two batches, only about half of them were completed. The only fully preserved boat is *XE-8*, which was sunk during gunnery exercises in 1952 and raised in 1973. Today, it is on display at Chatham Historic Dockyard in Southeast England. A modified variant of the *XE-Craft* with the designation *Stickleback*-class was built in the 1950s.

Closeup view of *XE-8*'s stern section. After 21 years underwater, the rudder has rusted away. (© Chatham Historic Dockyard Trust)

Operation *Struggle*

In August 1945, the midget submarines *XE-1* and *XE-3* executed a joint attack on Japanese heavy cruisers moored in the harbor of Singapore. While the former was ordered to attack the *Myōkō*, the latter was to destroy the *Takao*.

It took *XE-3* about 13 hours to get through the Strait of Johor and various harbor defenses to locate the camouflaged cruisers. Although the Japanese had several opportunities to spot the midget submarine, its crew reached the *Takao*, fixed limpet mines and dropped its two side charges close to the ship. *XE-3* then managed to withdraw and return to its towing submarine, HMS *Stygian*. In the meantime, *XE-1* was delayed by Japanese ships patrolling in the harbor. Therefore, its commanding officer realized that he could not reach the cruiser *Myōkō* before the mines already laid by *XE-3* would explode, as his target was two miles further into the harbor than the *Takao*. As a result, *XE-1* decided to drop its own charges under that cruiser as well before returning to its towing submarine, HMS *Spark*. While both boats were able to escape safely, the mine explosions damaged the already damaged cruiser *Takao* so severely that it was no longer operational for the duration of the war.

Year/s of construction	1944
Builder/qty completed	T. Broadbent & Sons/ca. 6
Length	53.25 ft (16.23 m)
Beam	18.86 ft (5.75 m)
Diesel engine	42 hp
Electric motor	30 hp
Propeller	1
Speed ↑	6.5 kn
Speed ↓	5.5 kn
Displacement	31 tons ↑/34 tons ↓
Range ↑	500 nm
Range ↓	82 nm at 2 kn
Crew	ca. 4
Diving depth	ca. 295 ft (90 m)
Armament	Various mines

Welman

Parallel to the development of the *X-Craft*, the smaller midget submarine type *Welman* with just one crewmember was also designed. The cylindrical vehicle with a centrally positioned conning tower could carry a 426 lb (193 kg) magnetic warhead at the front of the bow, which could be placed underneath the hulls of enemy ships. As the boat had no periscope, the small windows in the conning tower served as the only visual aid to navigation. The pilot sat in a watertight cockpit and therefore did not need a diving suit but wore a breathing mask. The propulsion system consisted of a 2.5 hp electric motor, which enabled a maximum speed of 3 kn to 4 kn (3.5 mph to 4.6 mph/5.6 kph to 7.4 kph) and a range of up to 36 nm (77 mi/67 km) (no precise data is available for overwater and underwater travel). During tests, the boat was able to reach a diving depth of nearly 300 ft (90 m), although only around 82 ft (25 m) was intended for operational use.

Design Flaws

The *Welman*'s major disadvantage from the operator's point of view was that it had no periscope like most other midget submarines. Without a way of viewing the surrounding area without surfacing, it was impossible to navigate covertly. Moreover, during surface travel the pilot's eye level was so close to sea level that objects more than two miles away were not visible. This put the *Welman* in danger of being detected and destroyed before finding a target.

The *Welman* midget submarines were only used once, when they were supposed to destroy a German floating dock in the Bergen harbor, Norway. One boat was captured by the Germans, whereupon the others abandoned the mission. (Royal Navy/Ministry of Defence)

A *Welman* midget submarine during trials in Australia. (National Archives of Australia)

Deployment

Although series production began after prototype testing at the end of 1942, the boats were not considered suitable for the tasks for which they were intended. Nevertheless, the decision was made to deploy them in Norway to destroy a German floating dock in Bergen harbor. Therefore, two British motor torpedo boats (MTBs) transported four *Welman* midget submarines (*W-45* to *W-48*) to the entrance of the fjord leading to Bergen, where the boats were released for their mission. When *W-46* became entangled in a submarine blocking net, it was forced to surface. After being discovered by a German patrol boat, the pilot, Norwegian Lieutenant B. Pedersen, was taken prisoner and his *Welman* was captured. As the three remaining midget submarines had lost their element of surprise because of this incident and were now in danger of being intercepted, they broke off their attacks and were scuttled by their pilots.

The three men were able to escape to the north with the help of the Norwegian resistance and were evacuated by a British MTB in February 1944. Pedersen survived the war in German captivity. After examining his boat, some of the design features were incorporated into German developments. The failure at Bergen prompted the Royal Navy to cancel any further *Welman* operations and to concentrate on the *X-Craft* and *XE-Craft* submarines. After the transfer of some *Welman* midget submarines to Australia, a few more trials were carried out there, but no operations ensued. Of the approximately 100 units built, no known complete boat has survived to this day.

A *Welman* with a detachable explosive charge on the bow before its trials on a lakeshore near London, England. (Ministry of Defence)

Year/s of construction	1942–43
Builder/qty completed	Morris Motors Limited/ca. 100
Length	17.25 ft (5.26 m) without explosives (20.5 ft or 6.25 m with explosives)
Beam	Unknown
Electric motor	2.5 PS
Propeller	1
Speed ↑	3–4 kn
Displacement	At least 1,984 lb (900 kg) (+ 507 lb/230 kg of explosives)
Range	36 nm
Crew	1
Diving depth	ca. 295 ft (90 m)
Armament	Explosives

Welfreighter

Motivated by the success of the *X-Craft*, the British Special Operations Executive (SOE), a special intelligence unit, designed a midget submarine designated *Welfreighter*. It was to be able to transport agents and saboteurs behind enemy lines or supply them on their missions. It was also to be used for reconnaissance on enemy coasts and to mine enemy sea routes. The *Welfreighter*, resembling a fishing smack in appearance, was to approach the area of operation at night, surface briefly and cover the final way submerged. By surfacing briefly at the drop-off point, the agents could then swim ashore for their mission and carry their equipment in watertight containers, while the *Welfreighter* withdrew to the open sea waiting submerged until it was supposed to pick up the men again at an agreed time and rendezvous point.

The boat would then return to its base under its own power or meet with a larger vessel, which would then serve as a transporter. For surface travel, the *Welfreighter* used a 44 hp Gardner 4LW diesel omnibus engine driving a four-bladed propeller, enabling a top speed of 7 kn (8 mph/13 kph) and a range of 900 nm (1,670 km). This radius could be increased by a further 1,400 nm (1,610 mi/2,600 km) with additional tanks (and fewer equipment containers). Underwater propulsion was provided by two 2 hp electric motors, driving two small propellers and enabling a speed of 2 to 3 kn (2.3 mph to 3.5 mph/3.7 kph to 5.6 kph; range unknown). The diving depth was up to 130 ft (40 m).

The *Welfreighter* could carry two crewmembers, up to four agents, and a ton of equipment. (National Archives of Australia)

The *Welfreighter* was powered by a diesel engine above water and an electric motor when submerged. (National Archives of Australia)

Appearance Like a Fishing Smack

The *Welfreighter*'s outward appearance resembled a conventional 37 ft (11 m) motorboat. The foredeck was raised to provide some headroom inside. It was fitted with small square viewports. It also housed a compass as well as a periscope. To disguise the *Welfreighter* as a fishing smack, a dummy mast and sail could be attached. To the rear of the main structure was a cargo well, fitted at the stern with a dropdown tailgate. This was capable of housing up to seven cylindrical containers holding equipment for use by agents or saboteurs. These drums could be floated out through the tailgate and towed ashore by the crew, either swimming or using a small inflatable boat.

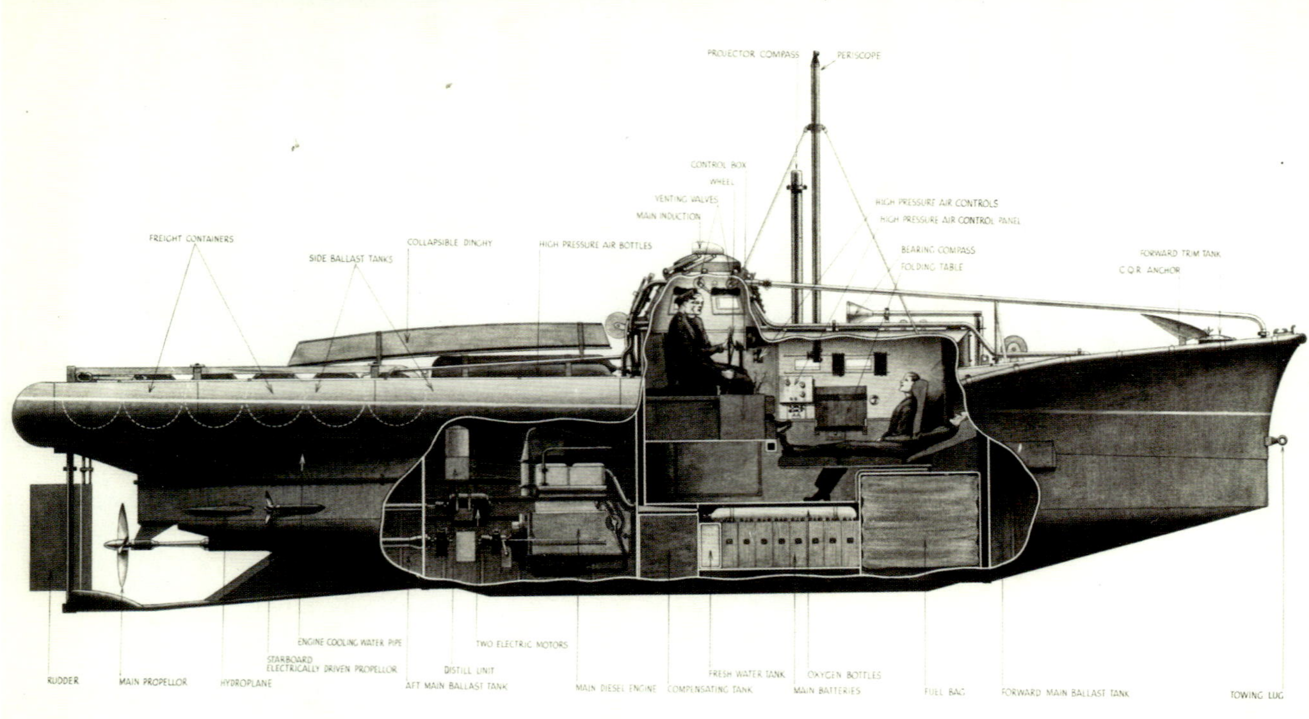

Simple drawing of the *Welfreighter* showing its interior spaces. (Ministry of Defence)

Deployment

After the construction and testing of two prototypes followed by a few modifications, series production began in 1944 at the vehicle manufacturer Shelvoke & Drewry Ltd. in Letchworth, England. At that time, however, it became clear that the *Welfreighter* would no longer be used in Europe due to the foreseeable German defeat. The idea of using it to mine German harbors, among other missions, was rejected, as the required 220 lb (100 kg) mine would have trimmed off the boat excessively. Finally, two boats were transferred to Fremantle in Australia. Although they carried out various trials there, they did not see any action before the end of the Pacific War (depending on the source). Although a total of around 100 units were built, no known complete boat has survived to this day.

Front view of a surfaced *Welfreighter*. Externally, it resembled a small motorboat or, if a dummy mast and sail were attached, a fishing smack. (National Archives of Australia)

Year/s of construction	1944–45
Builder/qty completed	Shelvoke & Drewry, Letchworth/ca. 100
Length	36.1 ft (11 m)
Beam	Unknown
Diesel engine	44 hp
Electric motor	2 × 2 hp
Propeller	1
Speed ↑	7 kn
Speed ↓	2–3 kn
Displacement	Unknown
Range ↑	900 nm without additional tanks
Crew	2 (+ 4 agents)
Diving depth	ca. 130 ft (40 m)
Armament	-

In Profile:
British Midget Submarines

X-Craft

The highly successful *X-Craft* was in development prior to 1939 and began series production in December 1942. Almost 52 ft (16 m) long and displacing up to 30 tons, the four-man crew consisted of the commander (navigation and operation of the periscope), the first lieutenant (ship's command and control), the engineer (monitoring of the boat's technical systems and maintenance of the drive), and the combat diver. The maximum speed was 5.5 kn (6.3 mph/10 kph) and the maximum range at a cruising speed of 2.2 kn (2.5 mph/4 kph) was around 82 nm (94 mi/152 km). The armament consisted of two side-mounted jettisonable bottom mines, each with 4,480 lb (2,032 kg) of Amatex explosives. The mines were dropped by a crank inside the boat and activated by a time fuze. The vessel was used to damage the *Tirpitz* at its berth in a Norwegian fjord, during Operation *Overlord* in a variety of duties, and to destroy Japanese heavy cruisers at anchor in Singapore harbor.

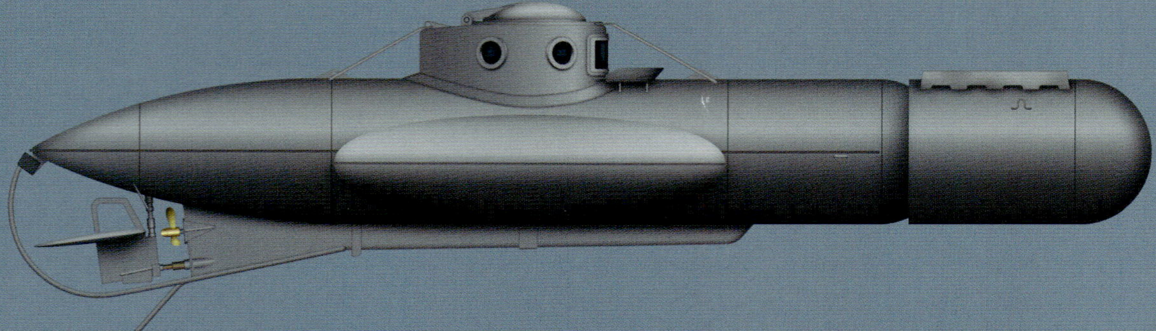

Welman

The *Welman* was only used once operationally, to destroy a German floating dock in the Bergen harbor, Norway. One boat was captured by the Germans, whereupon the others abandoned the mission. With a crew of one, the propulsion system consisted of a 2.5 hp electric motor, which enabled a maximum speed of 3 kn to 4 kn (3.5 mph to 4.6 mph/5.6 kph to 7.4 kph) and a range of up to 36 nm (77 mi/67 km). The cylindrical vehicle with a centrally positioned conning tower could carry a 426 lb (193 kg) magnetic warhead at the front of the bow, which could be placed underneath the hulls of enemy ships. The major drawback was that the vehicle had no periscope and was problematic to navigate.

Manned Torpedoes

Chariot

The severe damage to the two British battleships HMS *Queen Elizabeth* and HMS *Valiant* in the port of Alexandria caused by Italian *SLC*-type manned (human) torpedoes in December 1941 made the Royal Navy painfully aware of the potential of this weapon.

Following the recovery of several *SLC* wrecks and an intact one washed ashore near Gibraltar, a detailed investigation was carried out. Finally, British Prime Minister Winston Churchill commissioned the navy to develop similar small warfare weapons. The *SLC* served as a model, whose successful design was only modified to the extent that its concept could form a functional unit in combination with the British 21 in (53.3 cm) standard torpedo *Mark I* (the *SLC* was based on a standard Italian torpedo). The colloquial name for the *Mark I* became *Chariot*. As its development did not feature any significant innovations compared to the *SLC*, it was a kind of British counterpart with almost identical technology. The prototype, christened *Cassidy*, was used to carry out diving tests and to train future crews. At the same time, the diving suits and breathing devices specially developed for the torpedo riders were tested.

The British manned torpedo *Chariot* was largely a copy of the well-designed Italian *SLC*. (Royal Navy/Ministry of Defence)

The first *Chariots* (officially *Mark I Torpedo*) were delivered in June 1942. The total operating weight of 3,472 lb (1,575 kg) included the 660 lb (300 kg) warhead, which was detachable from the front section of the bow. After extensive sea trials, the improved version *Chariot II* (*Mark II Torpedo*) was soon developed. Introduced in the spring of 1944, this variant allowed the two torpedo riders to keep their legs inside the hull.

The *Chariot III* (*Mark III Torpedo*) was ultimately the most powerful of all three designs. It reached a top speed of 4.5 kn (5.2 mph/8.3 kph) (*Chariot I*: 2.9 kn to 3.3 mph/5.4 kph), had a greater range of 30 nm (64 mi/56 km) (*Chariot I*: 18 nm or 33 km) and could carry a 2,200 lb (1,000 kg) warhead. The means of transportation to the deployment area was inspired by the Italian method, so that the two submarines HMS *Thunderbolt* and HMS *P-311* were each fitted with two 26 ft (8 m) long pressure-resistant containers to house the *Chariots*. While the transportation on board speedboats was considered an emergency solution, a flying boat was only used once as a test, which turned out to be unsatisfactory.

A *Chariot* is lowered into the water. The controls were at the front. (Royal Navy/Ministry of Defence)

Deployments

Like the Italian manned torpedoes, the British *Chariots* were used in numerous operations in European coastal waters and occasionally in the Pacific. The first mission was directed against the German battleship *Tirpitz* in the Norwegian Asenfjord at the end of October 1942 (Operation *Title*). The means of transportation from England to Norway was a camouflaged fishing trawler with faked German documents. The two *Chariots* were hidden underneath a cargo of peat. Shortly before reaching the Norwegian coast, the boats were lowered into the water and attached under the hull. However, due to heavy seas, both *Chariots* broke free from their mounts and sank, causing the operation to be aborted.

On January 3, 1943, five manned torpedoes on board the mother submarines HMS *Thunderbolt* and HMS *P-311* were to attack the Italian port of Palermo in Sicily. On the way to the area of deployment, HMS *P-311* and its *Chariots* fell victim to an Italian torpedo boat. However, HMS *Thunderbolt* was able to launch its manned torpedoes, which sank the Italian light cruiser *Ulpio Traiano* and severely damaged the merchant ship *Viminale*. After the Italian heavy cruiser *Bolzano* fell into German hands following the Armistice of Cassibile in September 1943, it was sunk in the harbor of La Spezia in June 1944 in a combined attack by Italian *SLC* torpedo riders (now fighting on the Allied side) and British *Chariots* (depending on the source).

Transportation of several *Chariots* in pressure-resistant containers on the deck of a mother submarine. (Royal Navy/Ministry of Defence)

In early 1945, the British discontinued using their manned torpedoes in Europe, as there were practically no more German targets and the few remaining Kriegsmarine ships became now mostly victims of air raids. In the Far East, *Chariot* manned torpedo operations were also discontinued as the Royal Navy had heard (depending on the source) that the Japanese were torturing captured *Chariot* crews. By the end of the war, around 80 units of all three variants had been built. Although the Germans were aware of the *Chariot*'s technology and had access to the Italian *SLC*, they did not build such weapon systems but instead developed the *Neger* and the *Marder*. Today, some *Chariots* are preserved in various museums. The British Eden Camp Museum in North Yorkshire has a *Chariot* and a *SLC* on display.

The Secret Mission of *Tiny* and *Slasher*

On October 27, 1944, Sub-lieutenant Tony Eldrige and Petty Officer Sidney Woollcott boarded their *Chariot* named *Tiny* on a mission codenamed *Ceylon Secret Operation 51*. They were accompanied by another *Chariot* named *Slasher* crewed by Petty Officer W. S. Smith and Ordinary Seaman Bert Brown. Their objective was to sink the two 5,000-ton steamers *Sumatra* and *Volpi* near Phuket in Thailand, which had previously been raised by the Japanese. After being transported to Phuket by the submarine HMS *Trenchant*, both *Chariots* were launched at 2200 to navigate the final six miles to their target area under their own power.

Tiny arrived at 0030 (on October 28) at the steamer *Sumatra* to find out that the ship's hull had too many barnacles to secure the explosive warhead by using a magnet. As a result, Eldridge and Woollcott decided to attach a clamp to the bilge keel, tie the warhead to the clamp with a rope, set the timer for six hours, and return to their mother submarine HMS *Trenchant*.

Slasher found that their target, the steamer *Volpi*, was resting on the harbor bottom, thus making it impossible to attach their warhead underneath the hull. Instead, Bert Brown boarded the ship and placed the explosives in the engine room. After their safe return to HMS *Trenchant*, the men were ordered to scuttle their *Chariots* as the mother submarine's crew believed they had heard enemy propellers. This meant that there was no time to move the *Chariots* back into their transport containers. The explosives placed underneath the *Sumatra* and inside the *Volpi* eventually detonated and destroyed both steamers.

Depending on the source, the two scuttled *Chariots*, *Tiny* and *Slasher*, were either uncovered near Koh Dok Mai in the Andaman Sea following a tsunami in 2004 or located by scuba divers.

Year/s of construction	1942 (begin)
Builder/qty completed	Stothert & Pitt, Bath/ca. 80
Length	22.24 ft (6.78 m)
Beam	1.74 ft (0.53 m)
Electric motor	1.1 PS
Propeller	1
Speed	ca. 2.9 kn
Displacement	3,472 lb (1,575 kg) (incl. 661g lb/300 kg of explosives)
Range	18 nm
Crew	2
Diving depth	ca. 100 ft (30 m)
Armament	661 lb (300 kg) of explosives

Submersible Boats

Motorized Submersible Canoe

Parallel to the development of midget submarines and manned (human) torpedoes, the *MSC* (*Motorized Submersible Canoe*) was also developed by SOE. It was designed by Major Hugh Reeves as an underwater vehicle for a diver to attack ships in harbors. The 1.52 in (3.86 m) long steel construction was powered by a 5 hp electric motor and four 6-volt batteries. The maximum speed was 4.4 kn (5.1 mph/8.2 kph), with a range of up to 40 nm (46 mi/74 km) at a cruising speed of 3.1 kn (3.6 mph/5.7 kph).

The *MSC* had trim and ballast tanks and could dive to depths of up to 50 ft (15 m). The electric motor was located at the rear and the batteries were positioned in front of the driver. (U.S. Navy)

Depending on the mission, a second diver could ride in the front. A few *MSCs* have survived in museums to this day. (U.S. Navy)

For diving, the *MSC* had trim and ballast tanks in its hull. These were blown empty with compressed air for surfacing. The rudder and the two diving planes were operated using a joystick. The maximum operating depth was 50 ft (15 m). The pilot received his oxygen through a breathing apparatus with a head mask. A second diver could be seated next to him on the bow.

In late 1943, extensive testing and a comparison with the human (manned) torpedo *Chariot* and the midget submarine *Welman* took place. Compared to these, the *MSC* was easier and faster to build, and up to 15 units could be carried on the deck of a large mother submarine. It could also be transported to the deployment area by airplane and dropped from a low altitude shortly before reaching its target. In contrast to a self-sacrificial weapon equipped with explosives, with which the pilot rammed the target and died in the subsequent explosion, the *MSC* pilot was to bring his boat slowly up to the enemy ship, attach timer-activated magnetic mines to its hull and then return to safety by rendezvousing with a ship or submarine in an agreed area.

Deployment

Depending on the source, some *MSC* units with Norwegian crews are said to have carried out an unsuccessful attack on German shipping off Malmö, Sweden (which was neutral in World War II), during which some boats fell into German hands. There are also conflicting reports of an attack on Japanese ships in Singapore harbor, although it is not clear whether *MSC*-type submersibles or folding canoes (as surface craft) were used in this unsuccessful operation. In the summer of 1944, the American CIA received an *MSC* as a test boat, which served as the basis for the development of the modern "Swimmer Delivery Vehicle" ("diving scooter").

Year/s of construction	1943 (begin)
Builder/qty completed	Unknown
Length	12.66 ft (3.86 m)
Beam	2.26 ft (0.69 m)
Electric motor	5 hp
Propeller	1
Speed	4.4 kn
Displacement	ca. 595 lb (270 kg)
Range	Up to 40 nm at 3.1 kn
Crew	1–2
Diving depth	ca. 50 ft (15 m)
Armament	Explosives

5
Restoring and Operating a *Biber*

The task was as monumental as it was unique: restoring a German World War II *Biber* midget submarine, a rare and historically significant artifact, at the Royal Navy Submarine Museum in Gosport, England. It was a project that would test the limits of craftsmanship, knowledge, and teamwork in 2003. The submarine museum traces the international history of submarine development from antiquity to the present, and particularly the history of the Royal Navy Submarine service from its first boat, *Holland 1*, to the active nuclear-powered *Vanguard*-class. The institution is also home to the British World War II-era submarine HMS *Alliance*.

The *Biber* was restored to working condition by apprentices from Fleet Support Limited under the guidance of Ian Clark in 2003. The restoration featured in the British Channel 4's television program *Salvage Squad*, during which the craft was successfully test-dived in a flooded dry dock. (© Ian Clark)

A Unique Task

In early 2003, a *Biber* midget submarine arrived at the Royal Navy Submarine Museum. It had been carefully preserved but had suffered from decades of exposure to the elements, corrosion, and the ravages of time. Captured by the Allies, it had spent much of its existence in storage, with only minimal maintenance. Now, it would be up to a dedicated team of experts to return it to its former glory. Ian Clark, an expert in the restoration and conservation of maritime, industrial, and architectural objects and artifacts such as various historic submarines, ships, windmills, and machinery, was tasked with leading the restoration process. It was an opportunity to restore a piece of history with a unique set of challenges as the project required an interdisciplinary approach, involving not only mechanical engineering expertise but also insights into the materials and techniques used by the Kriegsmarine in constructing the *Biber*. The restoration team consisted of engineers, metalworkers, restorers, naval historians, and technicians, all of whom were deeply invested in the success of the project. The team worked in close collaboration, sharing their knowledge and expertise.

The restoration team faced a variety of challenges as they began the painstaking work of disassembling and restoring the submarine. Every part of the *Biber* needed to be assessed for damage, cleaned, and repaired, often using techniques that were as close as possible to those used during World War II. (© Ian Clark)

Corrosion, Structural Integrity, and Materials

The *Biber* had been exposed to the elements for decades, and its hull was severely corroded. The first task was to assess the structural integrity of the submarine. The restoration team quickly discovered that many sections of the hull had rusted through, making it difficult to maintain the vessel's shape and integrity. One of the primary challenges was ensuring that the restoration stayed true to the original *Biber* design. The Kriegsmarine used a variety of materials, including aluminum alloys and specialized steel, which are not commonly used today. Ian Clark and his team worked closely with historians and materials experts to source suitable replacements that would preserve the authenticity of the submarine.

Replacing the damaged sections of metal required expert welding and fabricating skills, as the original materials were no longer readily available. (© Ian Clark)

Engine and Propulsion System

The *Biber*'s engine and propulsion system, though simple in design, had suffered significant wear. The original 2.5 l Otto engine (from the Opel Blitz truck) with its 32 hp was restored, but not to operational condition. The original electric motor, however, was fully refurbished and drove the *Biber* during all the testing runs. The high- and low-pressure ballast systems were entirely rebuilt. The electrical systems, including all lighting and communication devices, were also in poor condition. Their restoration required careful work and a deep understanding of the submarine's original wiring and electrical layout. Many components needed to be rewired, and some modern electrical parts had to be adapted to fit the original design and function.

The main reason Ian Clark and his team did not restore the original engine to drive the *Biber* was to remove all risk and not repeat history—operating the submarine under battery power was the only safe option. (© Ian Clark)

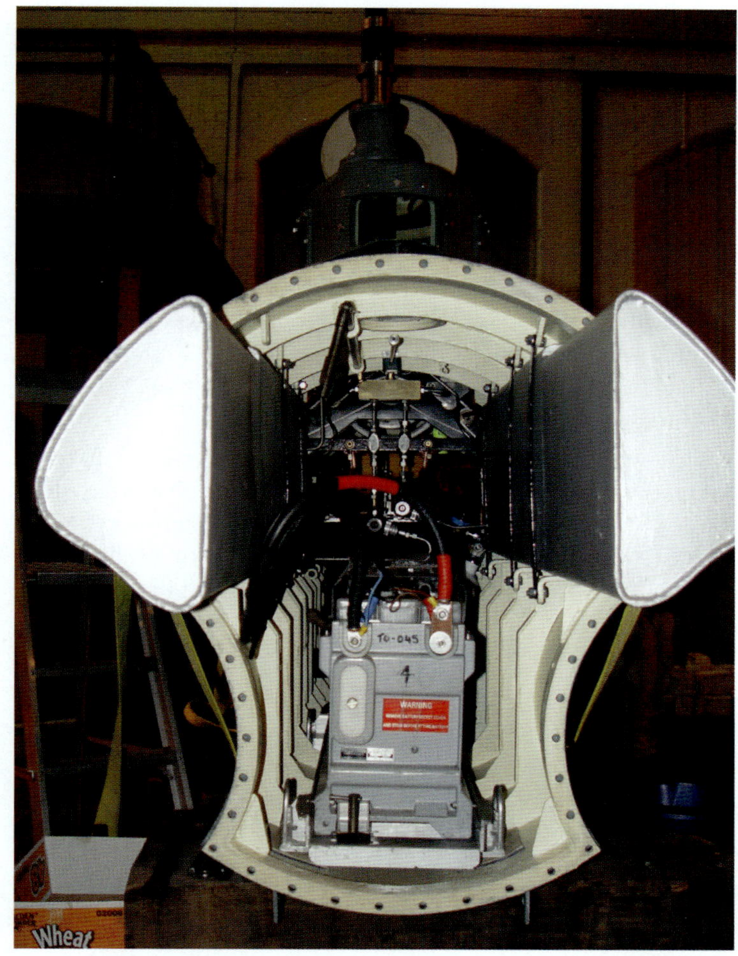

A high-performance modern battery unit which was the same physical size as the original bank of battery cells was borrowed from the Royal Navy to allow the *Biber* to be tested on the surface and underwater. (© Ian Clark)

The steering systems were entirely rebuilt. This included replicating a complete diving panel, controls, and the helm. (© Ian Clark)

Weather and Environmental Factors

The restoration was conducted in a museum environment, which presented its own set of challenges. The *Biber* had been in storage for a long time before arriving at the Royal Navy Submarine Museum, and there were concerns about how the temperature, humidity, and environmental factors might affect the materials and components of the submarine during the restoration process. The team worked in a controlled environment, but the natural aging of the materials still posed significant challenges.

Teamwork and Collaboration

Every team member brought their own unique skills to the table, whether it was in metalworking, electrical engineering, or historical research. The restorers worked closely with the engineers to ensure that each system was restored in harmony with the others. The metalworkers had to communicate with the historians to ensure that the materials and methods used for repairs were authentic to the original design. In turn, the historians worked together with the technicians to verify the specifications of each component, making sure that everything from the engine to the periscope was as accurate as possible. In addition to technical expertise, the team also had to demonstrate great patience.

Once the complex restoration was nearing completion, it was time to test the then-about 60-year-old *Biber* in order determine whether it was ready to take to the water once again. (© Ian Clark)

The Testing Phase

Ian Clark and his team meticulously prepared for the testing phase, ensuring that every aspect of the submarine had been checked and double-checked. The testing involved dry runs and water-based trials. First, the team tested the functionality of the electric motor and propulsion system in a dry environment, ensuring that everything operated smoothly. The team monitored the motor's performance, checking the pressure hull for leaks, unusual vibrations, or any signs of malfunction. The electrical systems were also checked during this phase, as they had to be fully operational for the submarine to function in the water.

Lowering the restored *Biber* into the water—probably for the first time since World War II. (© Ian Clark)

The *Biber* during a surface test-run in a flooded dry dock. Once all systems proved to work properly, it was time for a test dive. (© Ian Clark)

The Final Test Dive

Tom Heron was invited to pilot the *Biber* as he was one of the world's most experienced professional mini-submarine pilots. For example, he oversaw the rescue submarine *LR5* which dived to the sunken Russian submarine *Kursk* to try to rescue its crew in the Barents Sea in August 2000. Once the dry tests were successful, it was time for the ultimate challenge—the test dive. This was the final step before the *Biber* could be deemed fully restored and seaworthy. The team gathered at the museum's dock, with Tom at the helm of the midget submarine. The weather was calm, and the waters of the nearby harbor were still. The *Biber* was gently lowered into the water, and the moment of truth arrived. As Tom fired up the propulsion system, there was a collective sense of anticipation among the team. The submarine roared to life, and the *Biber* slowly began to move. The submarine maneuvered gracefully through the water, proving that the restoration had been a success. The final test dive was a success—the *Biber* descended slowly and began operating on battery power. Its electrical

During the test dive the *Biber* operated on battery power. One of the most important lessons Ian Clark and his team learned from the project was that the *Biber*'s design was far more advanced and sophisticated than recorded by most history books. (© Ian Clark)

systems worked perfectly, the propulsion was smooth, and when the submarine eventually surfaced, it seemed as capable as it had been during its brief operational period in World War II.

A comprehensive technical review of the basic hydrodynamic technical proficiency of the *Biber*'s hull design proved that, although history books have downplayed the potential success of the *Biber* project, the original technical design was in fact very efficient. The real failure within its design was not being able to provide a safe environment to protect the pilot from carbon monoxide poisoning from exhaust fumes generated by the Opel Blitz gasoline engine. The test dive marked the culmination of months of hard work. It was a moment of historical significance, as the *Biber* was now ready to take its place in the museum as a fully restored artifact preserved for future generations.

Tom Heron was the first pilot to operate an intact *Biber* since 1945. This *Biber* held by the Royal Navy Submarine Museum is believed to be the only operational World War II submarine in existence. (© Ian Clark)

6
Conclusion

The role and significance of World War II midget submarines constitute a unique chapter in the history of naval warfare. Though diminutive in size compared to conventional submarines, these small craft left a disproportionately large impact on strategic thinking, technological innovation, and special operations doctrine during and after the conflict. Their role in clandestine and high-risk missions, often bordering on the suicidal, underscores their symbolic as well as tactical importance. To understand their legacy, one must assess their operational deployment, the innovation they prompted, and the influence they had on future naval concepts.

In terms of technological significance, midget submarines catalyzed advances in miniaturized propulsion systems, stealth design, and undersea navigation. The necessity to maximize efficiency in confined spaces forced engineers to innovate compact yet effective systems for oxygen supply, control surfaces, and explosive payload delivery. Many of these innovations carried over into postwar submarine design and contributed to the development of modern special operations vehicles (SOVs) used by naval special forces. Midget submarines foreshadowed the integration of special operations with naval warfare, setting the stage for what would later become an essential aspect of asymmetric maritime conflict. Their missions often required extensive coordination with intelligence services, commandos, and support vessels, thereby fostering a more integrated and multidisciplinary approach to naval strategy. The courage and sacrifice of their crews also contributed to the cultural legacy of elite naval units, influencing the ethos of organizations such as the British Special Boat Service (SBS), U.S. Navy SEALs, and Italian COMSUBIN.

In the postwar period, the lessons learned from midget submarine operations informed the creation of more advanced and reliable diver delivery vehicles (DDVs) and swimmer delivery vehicles (SDVs). These craft retained the core philosophy of stealth, precision, and high-value targeting but incorporated significant improvements in comfort, safety, and operational reach. The Cold War saw a resurgence of interest in such platforms, especially among NATO and Warsaw Pact navies, for use in reconnaissance, sabotage, and infiltration missions.

From a legacy standpoint, midget submarines hold a dual place in history. On the one hand, they are remembered for their daring and often tragic missions, where technological shortcomings were often compensated for by the determination and bravery of their crews. On the other, they represent the nascent stages of a strategic shift toward covert and unconventional naval operations. Museums, memorials, and historical narratives continue to preserve their memory, offering both homage and critical reflection on their role.

In summary, World War II midget submarines played a specialized yet impactful role in maritime strategy. They pushed the boundaries of what was technically and humanly possible, often operating at the intersection of ingenuity and desperation. Though limited in tactical effectiveness, their psychological, technological, and doctrinal contributions have echoed through decades of naval innovation. As tools of stealth and surprise, they foreshadowed the modern era of precision warfare and remain an enduring testament to human ingenuity in times of extreme adversity.

The American USS *X-1* was an experimental midget submarine of the 1950s. It was used to explore how harbors could be defended against midget submarine or manned torpedo attacks but never entered series production. (U.S. Navy)

Further Reading

Bauernfeind, Ingo. *Typenkompass Kleinst-U-Boote 1939–1945*. Motorbuch-Verlag, 2019.

Benson, James, and C. E. T. Warren. *Above us the Waves: The Story of Midget Submarines and Human Torpedoes*. Pen & Sword Military Classics, 2007.

Burlingame, Burl. *Advance Force—Pearl Harbor*. Naval Institute Press, 2002.

Cocker, Maurice. *Royal Naval Sumbarines 1901 to 2008*. Pen & Sword Maritime, 2008.

Delgado, James P., Terry Kerby, Stephen Price, Maximilian D. Cremer, Hans K. Van Tilburg, Ole Varmer, and Russell Matthews. *The Lost Submarines of Pearl Harbor*. Texas A&M University Press, 2016.

Fock, Harald. *Marine-Kleinkampf-Mittel: Bemannte Torpedos, Klein-U-Boote, Klein-Schnellbote, Sprengbote. Gestern—heute—morgen*. Nikol, 1996.

Freidman, Norman. *British Submarines in Two World Wars*. Seaforth Publishing, 2019.

Kemp, Paul. *Midget Submarines of the Second World War*. Naval Institute Press, 1999.

Paterson, Lawrence. *Weapons of Desperation: German Frogmen and Midget Submarines of World War II*. Frontline Books, 2018.

Prenatt, Jamie, and Mark Stille, 2014. *Axis Midget Submarines: 1939–45*. Osprey Publishing, 2014.

Watkins, Paul. *Midget Submarine Commander: The Life of Godfrey Place VC*. Pen & Sword Maritime, 2013.

Index

Abbreviations—IJN: Imperial Japanese Navy; KM: Kriegsmarine; RM: Regia Marina (Italian Navy); RN: Royal Navy; USN: U.S. Navy